VICTIMS STILL

To Jennifer and
to my grandmother, Madeline

VICTIMS STILL

THE POLITICAL MANIPULATION OF CRIME VICTIMS

Robert Elias

University of San Francisco

SAGE Publications

International Educational and Professional Publisher

Newbury Park   London   New Delhi

For information address:

SAGE Publications, Inc.
2455 Teller Road
Newbury Park, California 91320

SAGE Publications Ltd.
6 Bonhill Street
London EC2A 4PU
United Kingdom

SAGE Publications India Pvt. Ltd.
M-32 Market
Greater Kailash I
New Delhi 110 048 India

Printed in the United States of America

Library of Congress Cataloging-in-Publication Data

Elias, Robert, 1950-
    Victims still : the political manipulation of crime victims / Robert Elias.
        p.   cm.
    Includes bibliographical references (p.   ) and index.
    ISBN 0-8039-5052-7 (cl.)   —ISBN 0-8039-5053-5 (pb)
    1. Victims of crimes—United States.   2. Criminal justice, Administration of—United States.   3. Reparation—United States.
I. Title.
HV6250.3.U5E46   1993
362.88—dc20   93-6511

93 94 95 96 10 9 8 7 6 5 4 3 2 1

Sage Production Editor: Tara S. Mead

Contents

Preface

T.S. Eliot wrote about times when "we had the experience but missed the meaning." This aptly describes what has happened with policy initiatives for crime victims over the last dozen years. By all appearances, this was a time when victims were finally taken seriously, when a flurry of new rights and services would lead to concrete improvements in victims' treatment. More important, these developments would reduce the victimization that people suffered from both crime and the criminal process.

Seeing those hopes fulfilled was the experience of sincere and hard-working victims' advocates in the 1980s and early 1990s. But the real meaning of these initiatives leaves us with a far more depressing reality. Most victim policy has fallen far short of the substantive changes we had hoped for, and criminal victimization continues at alarming levels. The revolution in crime control, which was built around restoring the victim's role, has not succeeded. There is evidence that officials never thought it should.

The real meaning of the last dozen years has everything to do with what most officials really want. They have wanted greater state control and a new dose of law-and-order crime policies. That is exactly what they have gotten. To achieve this end, they have been quite willing to use crime victims to help rally their cause. Behind the flurry of new policy and the very few victims' initiatives of any real substance, the real political agenda was to enhance conservative crime policies and social policies. As we will argue here, the real meaning of this experience is that victims have been politically manipulated. As a result, victims are victims still.

In the early 1980s, in *The Politics of Victimization* (Oxford University Press), I developed a theory—with the help of many others—about the likely manipulation of crime victims by government officials. While the theory seemed correct, based on limited information, I lacked the results of what was to become the apparent heyday for victim policy during the remainder of the 1980s and the early 1990s. Now the results are in, gathered not so much by me but by closer and more astute observers (whose research I will review herein) who had high hopes—and now have strong doubts—about whether the victims' movement has been successful after all. If the message of victims' manipulation was not absorbed before, then it will simply have to be sent again.

Many people will hate this book. Certainly I am critical of the conservatives who have held power these many years, but I am equally as critical of liberals. Criminal-justice personnel will not appreciate what I am saying even though I argue that they, too, have been frequently victimized by the law-and-order status quo. Dedicated victims' advocates will not want to hear what I have to say about the results of all their hard work; and most victimologists and criminologists will not agree with me that our work should be broader and take social conditions more seriously. Even some feminists might deplore my rejection of more force as the means to end male violence. Most important, victims might dislike this book, especially those who believe so deeply in the apparent gains that have been made over the years.

If I am wrong, then those who disagree will be little bothered by my faint words. If I am right, then perhaps these words will provide food for thought for fundamentally redesigning not only the victims' movement, but also our culture generally. We should not be fooled by existing victim policy, and rather than amiably bidding our problems goodbye—as if they either have been solved or cannot be solved—we should find ways to take those problems more seriously and embrace alternative policies that will get rid of them once and for all.

Although writing is often a lonely endeavor, I have several people to thank for their direct and indirect support. I am very thankful to Jennifer Turpin for her personal and intellectual support. I am grateful to my friends Bill Hoynes, Valerie Forman, Deirdre Burns, Maryanne Wolf, Andrea Oseas, and Susan Brison. I would like to thank my University of San Francisco colleagues Lois Lorentzen, Miriam Felblum, Richard Kozicki, Scott McElwain, Roberta Johnson, Tony Fels, and Else Tamayo. Many thanks also to the university's Faculty Development Committee and especially to Uldis Kruze for a grant that helped me complete this research. I appreciate the help provided by student assistants: Brenda Barrett, Michael Sullivan, William Faidi, and Michael Gunthorp.

I would like to thank colleagues around the country and world, including Kathleen Barry, Emilio Viano, Kevin Clements, Ezzat Fattah, Richard Quinney, Hal Pepinsky, Laurie Poore, Gary Marx, and Les Samuelson for both their support over the years and the stimulus they gave me for writing parts of this book. I appreciate Terry Hendrix, my editor, for taking an interest in the book and helping to make it better.

I would like to thank members of my family for their encouragement, including André Elias, August Elias, Patricia Barcel, and Madeline Foran.

Robert Elias
Berkeley, California

Everything that needs to be said has already been said. But since no one was listening, everything must be said again.
ANDRÉ GIDE

Americans never solve any of their problems; they just amiably bid them goodbye.
GEORGE SANTAYANA

But in a free country you cannot fool all of the people all of the time. Some of them will have a talent for fooling themselves, and they will insist on exercising it.
AUBREY MENEN

1

Still Victims After All These Years

Americans are so demoralized and self-degraded, you could throw them
into a stewpot and they'd stand up and salt themselves.

Gary Indiana

Promises, Promises

As I write, the City of Angels is burning. A dozen years ago, Ronald Reagan
launched new, get-tough policies that unleashed police departments across
the nation. Seven years later, George Bush defeated Michael Dukakis for the
presidency on the strength of his racist Willie Horton ads, further escalating
our violent response to crime.   — TRUE

These policies were rationalized in the name of crime victims. More law and
order—a tougher official stance—would protect victims and end the scourge
of crime. Almost four years after Bush's election, Los Angeles exploded in
reaction to years of official neglect toward the social victims of American
culture (Davis, 1992). The riots were sparked by yet another incident in a long
pattern of police brutality—a direct product of the White House's promotion
of official violence. Rather than convicting the offending officers—whose
videotaped beatings so conclusively proved their guilt—the Simi Valley jury
instead saw in Rodney King their worst fears: a black Willie Horton terror-
izing white cops and white communities. A city erupted; the president solemnly
deplored the violence.

The decade of the crime victim, launched by Reagan's 1981 presidential
task force, has instead produced more victims than ever, more fear of crime,   VERY TRUE

1

more racism and sexism, and more desperation (Messerschmidt, 1986). How does this help crime victims? Despite all the promises of the past dozen years, Americans are still victims of crime in unprecedented numbers, and are further from any real hope or solutions than ever before.

Who Benefits From Victim Policy?

We have crime, we need more force to stop it; only creates more problems

Crime will always be with us, we are told. There is only one way to confront it—with force. We need more police, firepower, and punishment, even though we already lead most other nations in exercising this kind of force. Even then, we can hope to achieve only so much.

With this philosophy, we have encountered another, almost predictable, escalation of crime, highlighted by increasing brutality, drug violence, domestic abuse, mass murders, abductions, sexual assaults, and hate crimes. As with previous crime waves, we have a set of household words for the current threats: Killeen and Howard Beach, Bundy and Salcedo, New Bedford and Central Park, Stockton and McDonald's, and so forth. Although they get less press than Zsa Zsa Gabor did a few years ago for slapping a police officer, these crimes do provoke official and media reaction. Yet the reaction is always the same: We must use more force, but after all, crime will always be with us.

In the face of each new crime wave, we get the same old answers from Democrats and Republicans, liberals and conservatives alike. Conservative Republicans such as Reagan and Bush are not the only ones supporting law-and-order strategies against crime. Recently, liberal Democrat Joseph Biden successfully sponsored a new Senate crime bill. It provides no new strategies; it only intensifies what has already failed: Biden tells us the bill is the "toughest ever." What passes as "new" crime policy repeats what we have tried before: building more prisons, beefing up police forces, curbing defendant's rights, increasing penalties. So, we launch yet another war on crime to accompany our failing war on drugs.

War on crime since war on drugs failed

People support these wars; but as they fail, their frustrations sometimes lead to aggression, which is the other side of the coin from the riots in south-central Los Angeles. People such as Bernhard Goetz, New York's so-called subway vigilante, launch their own violence against the problem, taking the law into their own, often racist, hands. Aside from vigilantism, people have few real alternatives to official crime policy. Victims, in particular, are frustrated.

In the last dozen years, we have tried something new to combat crime. We have shifted our focus from the crime and the criminal to the victimization and the victim. In the 1980s and early 1990s, victim policy has blossomed from the local to the national levels. Victims have been the subject of extensive new legislation that addresses victims' needs, rights, and services. We must help victims more; we must make them central again to law enforcement and criminal justice. But, to really address the victim's plight, officials predictably tell us, we must get tougher on crime and curb offender rights—even public rights generally: Increased police powers help victims the best. With this approach, we have witnessed the heyday of victim concern. Laws have proliferated, victim organizations have flourished, and victim rights have escalated. But what have the actual results been for victims?

Has legislation produced concrete improvements or has it only been symbolic? Have appropriations gone primarily to victims or instead to officials? Do new victim services help most victims or only the relative few? Has the victims' movement made a real difference for victims or has it been officially coopted? Have officials comforted victims or blamed them for their own victimization? Do harsher policies toward offenders really help victims or do they make victimization even more likely? Do crime policies help victims or do they use victims to perpetuate age-old, law-and-order ideologies? Do victims have more rights in practice or merely on paper? Are they helped or are they still victimized in the criminal process? Does victim policy help us aim at crime's root causes or does it divert us with crime's symptoms? Has the new victim policy been a sincere gesture or has it instead used victims for official objectives? Most important for victims, has victimization decreased or has it continued apace?

As we will see, it is hard to answer most of these questions positively for crime victims. Rather than offering real improvements, most victim policies still leave people victimized: by crime, criminal justice, and the political process. Victims are still manipulated after all these years.

The Political Manipulation of Victims

In the chapters ahead, we will examine how victims have been politically manipulated and what might be done to develop a more substantive and independent victims' movement.

First, we will review how officials define the crime problem. Their definitions help determine which victimization will—or will not—be taken seriously. This, in turn, profoundly affects whether victims are really taken seriously. Just as important, the public absorbs official conceptions of the crime problem largely through the media. We will show how the media, apparently lacking any memory about the anticrime strategies we have used repeatedly yet unsuccessfully, needlessly perpetuate official solutions that help increase rather than decrease victimization.

Next, we will examine the extensive new legislation that has emerged for victims, providing an array of apparent new rights and services. We will argue that those gains are far more apparent than real, and that victims have instead largely been used to promote conservative, law-and-order agendas. Then, we will examine the victims' movement, in particular, distinguishing between the "official" victims' movement—which reinforces establishment policies —and "hidden" victims' movements—which challenge the status quo, and therefore have been marginalized. Here, we can better see the weaknesses of the victims' movement in producing real change for both crime victims and other victims.

Officials repeatedly launch wars, purportedly to reduce victimization. By examining the government's most recent war on drugs, we will show how these wars not only fail to reduce crime, but also create significant new victimizations instead. Besides the violence of war, officials likewise advocate the violence of punishment. Victims are selectively enlisted in this crusade to fill ever more prisons. We will show, however, that victims do not necessarily want revenge and that harsh punishments create more, not less, victimization. In other words, victims are solicited to pursue policies that contradict their own best interests.

Finally, we will contrast the war strategy against crime with a peace strategy. We will see why officials really prefer war to peace, and how a more nonviolent social justice strategy can be much more effective in reducing victimization, both social and criminal. We will end with some proposals for how to create a new American culture and thereby develop a society that produces fewer victims.

We begin by examining the public's common understanding of the nature and causes of crime. Does this perception needlessly sell us short on what can be done to significantly reduce victimization? Are conventional strategies counterproductive? Because mainstream crime policy has repeatedly failed, why do we not know more about this failure, and why do we not hear more about the many alternatives that have been devised? Most Americans get their conceptions of crime and punishment from the media, yet the media uncritically convey official solutions that do not work. Why are the media so complacent, and how does the media's amnesia about the repeated failure of our many wars on crime help increase victimization?

2

Media Amnesia

ABETTING VICTIMIZATION

The press corps is like a pool of stenographers with amnesia.

I. F. Stone

The bias of the headlines, the systematic onesidedness of the reporting and the commentaries, the catchwords and slogans instead of argument. No serious appeal to reason. Instead a systematic effort to instill conditioned reflexes in the minds of the voters—and for the rest, crime, divorce, anecdotes, twaddle, anything to keep them distracted, anything to keep them from thinking.

Aldous Huxley

Crime Stories

True

By now it is commonplace to view victims as twice victimized: first by the crime and the criminal and then by the poor treatment they receive in the criminal process. But this ignores a larger victimization: the survival of policies that perpetuate rather than curb crime and violence and thus fail to prevent victimization in the first place.

Get tough, but no worthy results

Historically, U.S. crime policy has remained remarkably consistent, using "get tough" strategies to fight periodic crime wars. Just as predictably, this policy has failed: Victimization continues unabated. Policy makers shun the systemic changes needed for taking crime seriously and undoing the adverse

6

social conditions that generate most victimization. We might well understand policy makers' aversion to fundamental change: They would rather hide the historic failure of U.S. crime policy. How can they perform this sleight of hand?

As with most public policy, Americans learn about government crime policies largely through the media, including the press, which provides our window on public problems, on government strategies to solve them, and on how well they either fail or succeed. If Americans read the criminological literature, our crime policy's failure would be clear enough. Because most of us do not, we rely on the mass media to tell us whether our policies work, and, if not, why. How well have the media performed this public-information function?

The media have, with few exceptions, reproduced official, conservative law-and-order perspectives with little fundamental analysis of their success or failure (Bohm, 1986). The media have repeatedly covered and promoted wars against crime and drugs that inevitably fail but which the media periodically help resuscitate anew as if these wars had never before been fought—and lost. The media help abet criminal victimization by failing to hold policy makers responsible for strategies that predictably do not work; indeed, they make the problem worse. The media's amnesia, unwitting or not, encourages people to support policies that promote their own victimization.

When they are not getting their news from network television, millions of Americans rely on newsweeklies to keep track of their world. The commercials tell us to "Read *Time* and understand." But if we read *Time* or the two other major newsweeklies, *Newsweek* and *U.S. News & World Report*, will we really "understand"?

To find out what they have been telling us about crime and victimization, we have examined every general crime story appearing in these newsweeklies between 1956 and 1991 (see Appendix for the major headlines). Over these 35 years, a comprehensive portrait emerges of American violence and the U.S. government's policies to address it. What story does this coverage tell? How well does it serve victims?

Defining the Crime Problem

The newsweeklies faithfully reproduce government definitions of crime despite abundant evidence that officials define crime discriminatorily—by focusing primarily on lower- and working-class behavior—and exclude harms

[handwritten margin note top: rich more damaging than poors crime]

[handwritten margin note left of first line: how about corporate crime?]

such as corporate wrongdoing that are far more costly (in lives and lost or damaged property) than the harms they include (Elias, 1990; Reiman, 1984). As such, the newsweeklies help define, and also legitimize, the official version of the crime problem, its seriousness, and its cure (Fishman, 1978, 1980).

Accordingly, without a crime, there can be, officially, no victimization. Only those behaviors defined as crime are eligible to be treated as victimizations. And among those victimizations, only those pursued seriously by law enforcement get their due attention. Having not been defined as crime, the vastly more costly and threatening impact of corporate wrongdoing is not treated as victimization. Even harms such as domestic violence and sexual assault, formally defined as crime but only passively pursued by law enforcement, undermine the reality of the victimization involved. We are obsessed with drunk drivers, even though far more accidents are caused by safety defects and shoddily engineered automobiles, and we are obsessed with child abductions (even though quite rare) while we ignore the immensely larger problem of child abuse (Eliasoph, 1986). Without the media questioning crime categories, many genuine victims and victimizations are ignored: They are cast out of the public's consciousness and out of the realm of public assistance (Devitt & Downey, 1991; Lotz, 1988; Naureckas, 1991a).

[handwritten margin note left: corporate crime not seen as "bad"/deviant]

Even when the newsweeklies cover white-collar crime (as the endless scandals of the late 1980s made it almost impossible to avoid), the biases remain (Randall, Lee-Sammons, & Hagner, 1988). We never see the far greater victimization produced by these kinds of offenses. This crime is never portrayed as a structural or systemic problem (stemming, for example, from the injustices of capitalism) but rather only as a matter of deviant individuals such as Michael Milken or Ivan Boesky. *Newsweek*, for example, repeatedly argues that drug dealers and other common criminals must be "mercifully destroyed," yet claims that for white-collar criminals the "harshest penalty is the one they inflict on themselves" ("Getting Tough," 1988). Common criminals produce far less damage than white-collar and corporate criminals, yet while the newsweeklies clamor for the blood of the former, getting caught is punishment enough for the latter (Hutchinson, 1989). Unlike with street-crime coverage, suite-crime coverage shows no tearful victims, no outraged editorials, no fanciful theories of how Milken's or Boesky's laziness or bad upbringing caused their crimes (Hutchinson, 1990a).

[handwritten margin note left: scale very uneven]

Likewise, officials criminalize behavior that arguably produces no direct harm to others. While real victimization goes unrecognized, legislation against vice crimes punishes offenses that produce no direct victims. Worse, vice

[handwritten note bottom: attack poor when corporate crime cause more harm than one single street crime]

enforcement drains valuable resources (approximately one half in most urban police departments) away from pursuing harms that produce real victimization. These priorities do a disservice to victims; the media compound this disservice by legitimizing rather than questioning these priorities.

Aside from victimless crimes, the newsweeklies, like the government, conceptualize victimization as one-on-one offenses committed by strangers, even though most violent crime—and much property crime—actually occurs between people who know each other (Cumberbatch & Beardsworth, 1976; Roshier, 1981). Within that realm, the newsweeklies stress the exceptional over the commonplace: Sensational but unusual crimes get by far the most attention, even though this distorts the nature of most crimes (Garofalo, 1981). Alternatively, crimes such as mass murders get extensive play while largely missing the real story—that is, that most mass murderers are men, and most of their victims are women.

Finally, the media typically treat victims as innocent good people and accused offenders as guilty bad people, even though many victims have their own criminal records and even though many offenders have been victimized —by specific crimes and often by the unremittingly harsh environments of their past ("Crime Victims," 1983; "Victims of Crime," 1989; "What about the Victims," 1975; "What Crime Does," 1982). The newsweeklies, such as the so-called reality television cop programs, provide a misleading picture of the crime problem (Cavender & Bond-Maupin, 1991; Lee, 1978; Lichter & Lichter, 1983; Pandiani, 1978; Parenti, 1986; Sherizen, 1978).

Who Are the Criminals?

Who we conceptualize as criminals relies first on how we have bounded our understanding of crime. With the media's help, therefore, we consider as criminals only those kinds of people committing the behaviors defined— officially or otherwise—as crime. Thus, we begin already with a biased sample of those people who cause harm.

But within that realm, do we really consider as criminals all the people who commit these acts—or only some of them? Even after ruling out those offenders whose harms, although serious, are not officially defined as crime, the newsweeklies only conceptualize as criminals a portion of those who commit official crimes. The newsweeklies take their cue from law enforcement, not reporting about all those who commit crimes but rather about those who

VERY TRUE

police departments emphasize and pursue as criminals, whether they are responsible for most crime or not. Members of minorities are the ones arrested in
most drug busts even though whites consume more illegal narcotics. Drug
laws and crackdowns have historically followed the changing drug-use
patterns of minorities, not the seriousness of the drugs themselves; criminality is largely manufactured for certain groups (Duster, 1970). The newsweeklies periodically and condescendingly lament "black-on-black crime," while
ignoring its causes as well as the higher level of crime committed by whites
against whites (Hutchinson, 1990a). The media do practically nothing to
second-guess our conventional conceptions of criminals and criminality.[1]

Who, then, do we find portrayed as criminals in the newsweeklies? Well,
they have "changed" over the last 35 years: First, they were the negroes.
Then they were the blacks. And now they are the African-Americans. Who
do we see described and pictured in the newsweeklies crime coverage? Mostly
African-Americans and other nonwhites, even though these groups do not
commit the majority of crimes—even as selectively defined (Reed, 1989;
Smith, 1992).

We see blacks being pursued, booked, questioned, and hauled off to prison
(Hutchinson, 1989). In contrast, the newsweeklies describe and picture victims
as mostly white people, even though minority groups are arguably the
biggest victims. Consider, for example, the flood of coverage for the Carol
Stuart murder case, during which the media cheered on the Boston police's
"search and destroy" mission to root out the accused black man. Never mind
that she was actually murdered by her husband, Charles Stuart, a far more
likely suspect, who made up the black assailant story (Kopkind, 1990). And
never mind that the real story here was yet another woman victim of domestic
violence (Margaronis, 1990).

Interesting

This pattern holds true with only one apparent exception: When a black
man is accused of victimizing a black woman. Then it is sexism rather than
racism that predicts the outcome. Consider the vicious victim blaming by the
media against Anita Hill despite the formidable evidence of sexual harassment she supplied against U.S. Supreme Court nominee Clarence Thomas
(Pollitt, 1991b).

What emerges is a pattern of discrimination by which the newsweeklies
conceptualize criminals as black people and crime as the violence blacks do
to whites. Yet it did not prevent *Newsweek*, for example, from running a story
after the 1992 Los Angeles riot that claimed the public, politicians, and the
media have engaged in a "conspiracy of silence" by not admitting that they

associate crime with black faces (Mabry & Thomas, 1992)! No wonder that we have such a race problem in the United States. So what do people learn from the newsweeklies about who the criminals are? They are African-Americans (McPherson, 1992).

Heroes and Victims

Who confronts this scourge of African-American crime? Accurately enough, the newsweeklies show us white police officers at the front lines. Do the newsweeklies lament the suspicious racial confrontation this represents? Do they question what pits black offenders against not only white victims but also white cops? No, instead they let readers draw the inevitably racist conclusions about blacks, the breeding grounds for which the media itself have created.

Police officers are invariably portrayed as victims. But victims of whom and what? According to the newsweeklies, police are victimized by violent crimes and vicious people, even though almost all crimes occur when officers are not around ("Police Under Attack," 1970). The newsweeklies also tell us that police are victimized by institutional constraints: First, police do not get enough resources, even though law-enforcement appropriations actually keep rising. Second, police are handcuffed by soft and liberal courts that restrict police practices and allow rights technicalities to create a revolving door in the criminal process ("Court Rulings Frustrate," 1959; "Courts Too Easy," 1972; "When the Police Blunder," 1982; "Why Criminals Go Free," 1976). This set of beliefs enters the public consciousness despite abundant contradictory evidence (Rudovsky, 1988).

In contrast, the media omit other perspectives on the relationship between the police and victimization (Mishra, 1979). For example, despite the persistent cases of police brutality and misconduct over the years, almost no reports claim the police cause victimization ("Cops and Cameras," 1991). Even the recent videotaped beating of Rodney King by Los Angeles police officers produced only mild rebukes from the newsweeklies (Hutchinson, 1991). Rather than being examined as a systemic problem, the media focus on deviant officers and the frustrations of police work ("Video Vigilantes," 1991).

The newsweeklies also take conventional get-tough crime policies for granted. No consideration is given to whether victimization of the police might come not so much from actual crimes and offenders but rather from

policies that ignore crime's fundamental causes and which unnecessarily perpetuate violence in American society. Law-and-order crime policies that pursue
violent, counterproductive solutions and routinely place law enforcers in the
resulting crossfire may victimize the police most of all.

To complement their portrayal as victims, the newsweeklies also often treat
police officers as heroes ("How Supreme Court Is Curbing Police," 1965;
"What the Police Can and Cannot Do," 1970). Cops are merely neutral civil
servants just trying to do their job. If they get out of hand, it is only the necessary by-product of the unsolvable threat they face. Nevertheless, the newsweeklies do not always portray the police as successful. Indeed, the articles
fluctuate wildly between police forces' success and their failure, often drawing
diametrically opposed conclusions within only a few months. A reader would
be hard-pressed to really know whether progress was being made. Even so,
police officers are no less the heroes when they fail; instead, they are only
overwhelmed by the impossible task before them. True enough, but one
wonders why the newsweeklies never really examine why the police are
fighting a losing battle. Could it be because we have basically pursued the
wrong policies all these years? To read *Time*, *Newsweek*, and *U.S. News &
World Report*, one would never know—or even think to ask.

Savages and Bleeding Hearts

Law enforcement routinely fails, but police officers do not cause crime.
So what does? According to the newsweeklies, crime is caused by evil people
and misguided do-gooders. People are victimized because bad characters
inevitably exist. Some people are naturally evil or are led down the path of
wrongdoing by permissiveness and bad upbringings. Thus, we will always
have criminals; all we can do is remain as vigilant as possible against them
("Are Criminals Born?" 1985; "Genetic Traits," 1985; "Is Nature to Blame?"
1986; "Living with Crime," 1972).

But victims beware! Vigilance cannot be maintained if we leave the task
to the do-gooders in our society. The newsweeklies tell us that bleeding-heart
liberals are the ones who undermine the toughness needed to do the job.
Instead of the revolving door, we need harshness—including capital punishment, the only language the "savages" and "monsters" among us understand
—not compassion and rights ("Behind Violence," 1981; "Criminal Is Living,"
1965; "Drug Kingpin," 1988; Fraser, 1990; "Reconsidering Suspects' Rights,"

1976; "Seeing Justice," 1986; "When the Guilty," 1989; "Why Justice?" 1989). This we are told even though the United States has long had the world's highest incarceration rate and the second highest (after South Africa) severity in its penalties (Elvin, 1991; Mauer, 1991). Unchallenged by the media, the myth of the revolving door can affect not only crime policy, but also presidential elections as demonstrated by the so-called Willie Horton ads used against Michael Dukakis. Never mind that George Bush supported identical furlough programs sponsored by Texas and the federal government.

The newsweeklies do not really consider the "causes" or "sources" of victimization at all. Even when using those words, at most they only examine crime's symptoms ("Attacking the Source," 1989; "Behind the Violence," 1978; "Is There a Sick Society?" 1967; "Stop Drugs," 1986; "Striking at the Source," 1986). Rather than examining whether something might be wrong with our laws, our society, or our fundamental institutions, the newsweeklies conceptualize crime as an entirely individualized problem: Everyone has the opportunity to avoid becoming a criminal. It is the individual's choice, except, of course, for those irretrievably evil people among us who must simply be put away.

How, then, can we prevent crime? According to the newsweeklies, we must provide endless resources to law enforcement, abandon rights technicalities that handcuff the police, toughen our penalties and build more prisons, harden criminal targets, enlist widespread community cooperation, change our careless life-styles, curb our permissive society, and experiment with exotic reforms such as bicycle cops, preventive detention, law-enforcement ROTC, and boot camp or minefield prisons ("Experiments," 1989; "ROTC," 1983).

Covering Victims

When the government launches its periodic crime campaigns, the media dutifully serve as its publicist, even though officials often promulgate distorted conceptions of the crime problem and predictably counterproductive solutions. The newsweeklies have routinely joined these crusades (Gitlin, 1989). Increasingly, they have been launched in the name of victims: we have to get tough (as if we had not been before) to help victims. People must be willing to forego their rights to secure greater security against victimization ("Back to Basics," 1986; "We Need Drastic Measures," 1989). Yet little of this helps victims in any way.

The policies pursued do not work and arguably help perpetuate victimization rather than reduce it. Certainly, victims gain nothing here. Just as bad, victims often end up mistreated, first by officials and then by the media, even while they are being lauded in these campaigns. Officials routinely release the names of victims, even in sensitive cases—such as sexual assault and domestic violence—where doing so subjects victims to dire consequences (Carr, 1991; Fitzgerald, 1990). Officials also regularly blame victims for the offenses committed against them. Despite sporadic sensitivity training, law enforcers still accuse victims of being in the wrong place, dressing in the wrong way, saying the wrong thing, and so forth.

Instead of challenging this, the media largely do the same thing. The newsweeklies often release the names of victims. Although they routinely block stories and withhold information about things such as government or corporate wrongdoing (Solomon & Lee, 1991), suddenly it becomes part of the public's "right to know" when it comes to naming victims (Devitt & Rhodes, 1991; Pollitt, 1991a). Even sexual assault victims are now being named, such as in the recent William Kennedy Smith case (Carr, 1991; Ledbetter, 1991; Naureckas, 1991c). *Newsweek*, for example, did not join media outlets such as NBC and *The New York Times* in directly naming the woman, yet it nevertheless covered the case with an article by a *Newsweek* writer who advocated the naming of victims (Kaplan, 1991) despite the obvious additional victimization it produces (Dworkin, 1991). Like officials, the newsweeklies also often blame victims for their victimization, either explicitly or implicitly, usually by simply and unabashedly quoting the official line (Udovitch, 1991).

Alternatively, victims get the same message indirectly when the newsweeklies periodically print the kinds of things "you can do to prevent crime" (e.g., see "Theft-Proofing," 1988; "Tips," 1986). This resembles the "public service" advertisements that try to tell us that litter is our primary environmental threat: "People start pollution, only people can stop it." It is not greedy corporations, unregulated industrial capitalism, or a flagging political system that cause pollution or crime, but rather careless individuals who do not take the proper precautions or who do not pitch in enough to help benevolent and beleaguered officials. So if it is not simply evil savages and misguided do-gooders who cause crime, then it is also victims.

Victims/offenders are bad unless they are

Tempted by the Devil

But some kinds of crimes might have still other causes. What causes drug crimes? The newsweeklies tell us that in addition to all the normal suspects, foreigners also cause crime. The analysis begins with the altogether dubious assumption that drugs cause crimes instead of the greater likelihood that drug laws and drug enforcement cause crimes. Because the newsweeklies treat drug use as a stimulant to crime, despite evidence to the contrary, drug enforcement—as a policy—escapes any serious examination. Then, because drugs are, by definition, bad in themselves—even though we have only a half-sober society consuming dozens of legalized drugs—and because drugs are assumed to produce more crimes, the newsweeklies have no alternative but to focus our attention on the sources of those drugs. This leads us inevitably to foreigners and foreign nations as the cause of crime ("U.S. Mission," 1986).

Accordingly, the newsweeklies have paraded before us a series of foreign culprits. Some foreigners, such as the "Red" Chinese and the Cubans, are treated as inherently evil, as monsters trying to undermine our way of life for ideological purposes—despite little evidence to support the notion that these nations are major drug sources ("Dope from Red China," 1956). When officials and the media could no longer deny the growing addiction rates among U.S. soldiers both during and after their tours in Vietnam, it was only the evil Viet Cong to blame ("Fresh Disclosures," 1970). Not mentioned was the long-standing involvement of the Central Intelligence Agency (CIA) in Southeast Asia's drug trade (McCoy, 1984).

Other foreigners, including some of our purported friends, are treated less as evil and more as simply incompetent ("Has Mexico Matched Up?" 1985). We read reports not only about Burma, Turkey, Bolivia, and Peru, but also and especially about Colombia, Mexico, and Panama ("Wanted," 1988). None of these nations seems to be able to do the job; the United States has no choice but to intervene to lend a helping hand. This may even require a U.S. military invasion such as the attack against Panama to kidnap Manuel Noriega; never mind that Noriega ran drugs for the CIA and the White House and that his U.S.-engineered successors also head Panamanian banks that launder drug money. It is not U.S. policy toward these nations, whether friends or foes, that promotes the drug flow and victimizes other peoples, but rather it is the irresponsibility or evilness of foreigners that causes the problem. Sometimes only force can make foreigners see how much they are victimizing us here in the democratic United States.

Experts Right and Wrong

> In ways which journalists themselves perceive only dimly or not at all, they are
> bought, or compromised, or manipulated into confirming the official lies: not
> the little ones, which they delight in exposing, but the big ones, which they do
> not normally think of as lies at all, and which they cannot distinguish from the
> truth.
>
> Andrew Kopkind

How do we know what causes crime and victimization? How do we know
who to blame? How to do we know how to respond? We know because the
newsweeklies ask the experts. But which experts do they consult, and are they
really experts? In the past 35 years, the newsweeklies have printed dozens
of anticrime speeches, and have run lengthy, one-on-one, "exclusive" interviews
with people who supposedly have the answers.

When we examine these interviews, we find the experts often unqualified,
the expertise routinely dubious, and the perspectives invariably conservative. To begin with, the ideologies presented are almost unremittingly right-
wing. In more than 85 interviews completed by the newsweeklies over the
last 35 years, only one expert—Alan Dershowitz—fell left of the middle of
the political spectrum, and Dershowitz is a man who is regarded as increasingly conservative. Indeed, these interviews hardly reveal anyone we might
even call a *moderate* on crime policy. Virtually all the interviews were done
with people who hold strongly conservative, if not reactionary, law-and-
order views on crime control. No wonder the underlying sources of crime
receive almost no consideration by the newsweeklies.

Aside from ideology, where do the experts come from? Almost all hold
government positions, usually in some aspect of law enforcement. Only 11
were not working for the government when they were interviewed. In other
words we can ask, *who* do the newsweeklies regard as the experts? And
who, therefore, do we readers come to regard as the experts? Government
officials. But could it be that these officials might not be entirely objective
about the efficacy of conventional crime policy—policies for which they
are often personally responsible? Such a notion never seems to occur at the
newsweeklies.

What government officials, specifically, do we hear from? First, we hear
the most from various heads of the Federal Bureau of Investigation (FBI),
led prominently by one interview after another with J. Edgar Hoover. Second,
we hear from various conservative senators, led by John McClellan, who

fueled an entire career based on get-tough crime policies. Third, we hear from several U.S. attorneys general, with the notable omission of the only genuine liberals in the last 35 years: Ramsey Clark and Bobby Kennedy. Instead, we read interviews with attorneys general such as Richard Kleindeinst, William French Smith, and, repeatedly, John Mitchell—before his own imprisonment for violating the law. Somehow, the only presidents who have had sufficient expertise to warrant interviews have been Richard Nixon, who was forced to resign for violating the U.S. Constitution, and Ronald Reagan, who presided over the most criminally indicted administration in U.S. history.

The newsweeklies have interviewed many police superintendents and battle-weary police sergeants, various get-tough district attorneys from many of the United States' largest and most crime-ridden cities, and a sampling of conservative judges, ranging from local judges such as Seattle's William Long to Supreme Court justices such as Warren Burger, who invariably condemn their own weak-willed colleagues. Interviews were routinely conducted with the heads of various divisions within the Department of Justice such as the Criminal Division and the Law Enforcement Assistance Administration (LEAA); with affiliated agencies such as the Customs Bureau and Civil Aviation Security; and with various drug enforcers such as the Drug Enforcement Administration (DEA), the National Institute on Drug Abuse (NIDA), the Federal Bureau of Narcotics, and the Department of State's International Narcotics Bureau.

Who counters the overwhelmingly uniform and conservative government perspective provided by these official experts? Those interviewed outside government have included a handful of psychiatrists, lawyers, law professors, sociologists, college presidents, and members of the clergy. Virtually without exception, these voices echoed instead of challenged official explanations for crime and what to do about it. The psychiatrists attributed crime to evil individuals. The sociologists claimed we were too soft on crime. And the clergy has decried our permissiveness and declining moral fiber.

Whether officials or not, most of those interviewed by the newsweeklies would be hard-pressed to demonstrate their expertise on the crime problem they were so eager to discuss. Nor do they have the slightest understanding of victims or victimization. Somehow, expertise seems confirmed simply by virtue of appointment or general status in society, even if the "expert" has had little or no background in the field. For those few who really did have an appropriate expertise, the newsweeklies could not have chosen sources more strongly supportive of the status quo. If the newsweeklies were going

VERY
TRUE
WHY
NOT?

to repeatedly interview conservative or reactionary criminologists such as James Q. Wilson and Fred Inbau, then why not also interview liberal or progressive criminologists such as William Chambliss and Elliott Currie?

What the so-called experts show in these interviews is their unwillingness or inability to progress much beyond mouthing the usual cliches about preventing crime. The media reproduce, indeed embody, the consistently unsuccessful crime policies we have been using for most of this century. Rather than challenging the persistent failure of law-and-order crime policies, the newsweeklies not only endorse them but also promote their "exclusive" interviews as offering new, never-seen-before ideas to battle crime.

And Now for Something Totally Different

> In our country people are rarely imprisoned *for* their ideas because we are already imprisoned *by* our ideas.
>
> Marcus Garvey

Summary

We can see even more glaring examples of old ideas paraded as brilliant new solutions when we examine the newsweeklies' coverage of wars on crime and drugs. We are all familiar, of course, with the crime war and drug war launched by both the Reagan and Bush administrations. Because we are apparently incapable of "just saying 'no,' " the government has been forced to launch a no-holds-barred police and military assault on the crime and drug problem.

With few exceptions, the newsweeklies have accepted these wars; indeed, they have adopted them for their own, running one story after another that breathlessly reports the escapades of our caped crusaders (Giordana, 1990; Levine & Reinarman, 1987; Naureckas, 1991b). Even the mainstream media have wondered whether they have been overdosing on drug coverage ("Is TV News," 1990; Henry, 1986). Wars against crime and drugs have not only been embraced, but also been presented as new ideas, as policies we have never tried before ("Blueprint," 1979; "How to Win," 1968; "New Era," 1990; "What to Do about Crime," 1967). Because we have never before tried declaring war on the problem, we now have a great new opportunity to see a policy that finally works.

Unfortunately, we *have* launched wars against crime and drugs before— repeatedly —at least a few in each of the last three decades. Could these wars

repeation of things already done

have been launched without the newsweeklies knowing? Or have such wars been conveniently thrown down the memory hole?

When we examine the newsweeklies' crime coverage since the 1950s, we discover that they knew all about the government's previous wars on crime and drugs. Indeed, when each new war was launched, the newsweeklies performed as faithful cheerleaders for the policy. Yet each time, the newsweeklies reported the new wars on crime or drugs as if it had not covered the previous one—just a few years earlier. Crime stories are repeatedly recycled: Contents and headlines have been almost interchangeable, both within and among the newsweeklies, for more than three decades. *U.S. News & World Report* even ran the identical picture of a Los Angeles narcotics arrest twice —10 years apart! [Compare "Court Rulings" (1959) and "'Growing Menace'" (1971).] The extraordinary amnesia of this coverage has helped conceal the fact that each of these wars has failed—and failed miserably. Wars on crime and drugs do not work; they are usually counterproductive, producing more, not less, victimization (Cipes, 1968).

Suppose victims and the general public knew about the persistent failure of crime wars, each using virtually the same strategies as the one before (Sacco, 1982). Would that change how willingly the public would support these policies? Would better information make any difference? Do the newsweeklies and other media have any responsibility to provide this kind of information? Can we expect the public to have any memory if the media on which it relies have a persistent amnesia of their own (Comstock, 1981)?

People Fight Back

Because, according to the newsweeklies, the people are ultimately responsible for preventing crime, it is not surprising that these magazines would prominently feature ways in which ordinary citizens have "fought back" ("Fighting Back," 1989; "Public Fights Back," 1987; "Street Crime," 1985).

First, the citizenry's heightened fear of crime must be stressed ("Flames of Fear," 1987; "Fear of Crime," 1980; "Murder," 1989; "White Fear," 1979), an issue quite apart from whether the newsweeklies' own coverage artificially enhances that anxiety (Gordon & Heath, 1981; Stroman & Seltzer, 1985; Warr, 1990). Next, citizens are portrayed as being at the "end of their tether" and usually disgusted by the criminal-justice system's unwillingness to get tough on criminals ("War on Crime," 1975). Then, we learn how citizens have taken matters into their own hands.

How do people take control of the crime problem? First, they never resort to vigilantism because that would be going too far—even if the newsweeklies have repeatedly created the environment for just such a response. Instead, citizens adopt various self-protection strategies. Most important, they must take or buy various security measures, including guard dogs, armed attendants, lighting systems, foolproof locks, walkie-talkies, and dozens of other crime-control gadgets ("Making Sense," 1986). They must also take self-defense classes and learn avoidance behavior; that is, they must learn how to substantially reshape their lives and life-styles to steer clear of crime ("Public Safety," 1970). Citizens must form or join crime-control organizations, such as Crime Stoppers, Neighborhood Watch, or citizen patrols ("Crime Stoppers," 1979; "Only the People," 1970). And they must systematically monitor judges, police officers, and other officials to make sure they are being tough enough on criminals ("When Citizens Mobilize," 1980). All of this, the newsweeklies tell us, is not only what citizens do, but also what they *must* do to check crime.

Never mind that vigilantism does routinely emerge from this environment and that crime-control gadgets are either too expensive or do not work—while offering huge profits for the security industry. Never mind that these strategies do nothing to address and eliminate crime's fundamental sources and instead ask us to adapt to an inevitably criminal society ("Future Cities," 1970). Never mind that most citizen organizations are created and run by officials as public relations gimmicks, adopting traditionally unsuccessful crime-fighting strategies. Never mind that programs such as Crime Stoppers and Neighborhood Watch have little or no impact on reducing crime (Carriere & Ericson, 1989; Hentig, 1984). And never mind that we already have the world's toughest criminal-justice system.

The newsweeklies coverage of Bernhard Goetz, the so-called subway vigilante, illustrates well the media's perspective. The newsweeklies claimed that they deplore vigilantism, and yet their stories, constructed over the long history of this case, helped justify precisely that response. It is wrong, the newsweeklies tell us, to pull a gun and start shooting people who you imagine might want to victimize you, but, after all, how else can we expect a frustrated citizenry to react? It is wrong to make Goetz into a hero, but we cannot help it if New Yorkers and other Americans think this guy is great; we are just reporters. It is wrong to promote racism, but this was a matter of black youths with a criminal record who might have been planning to attack a white man—who also has a criminal record, but because that is irrelevant we will not report it. It is wrong for people to violate gun-control laws, but how can you blame people for trying to protect themselves? It is deplorable that people are victimized, but who, after all, are the real victims here? It is horrible the level of crime this kind of case reveals, but let us focus only on the individuals involved and ignore the systemic roots of the problem (Rubin, 1986). With the newsweeklies' encouragement, the people do fight back—and with everything except that which would seriously address the problem. With the media's social construction of the crime problem, how else could people be expected to respond (Graber, 1980)?

People can and should take control of crime prevention from an establishment that has historically shown itself unwilling or unable to take crime seriously. People can and must fight back. But they can adopt alternative, more successful strategies only if they address crime's structural sources, which are embedded in the American system (Elias, 1993b). Successful crime reduction requires a fundamental change in American culture: a substantial reform of our unequal and unjust political, economic, and social structures. People can launch that change in their own communities, but only through organizations controlled by them, not by officials who have everything to lose from such changes (Brady, 1981). And where would the citizenry get the information it needs to understand crime's real roots and to successfully respond? Presumably from the newsweeklies and other media that, if they were performing their public function, would readily assume that role (Barak, 1988). This is a far cry from the media's current function as legitimizers of conventional crime policy (Lapham, 1989).

Language of War

In our repeated wars on crime and drugs, "war" is not merely a strategy, it is a cultural psychology. Taking a problem seriously—even if the resulting policies demonstrably fail—requires us to go to war. We are a culture of violent solutions, even if our violence—from the Persian Gulf to our city streets—solves nothing at all (Elias, 1993a). We "solve" the violence of crime by committing more violence, however counterproductive. When random, official violence will not suffice, only the organized violence of war will do (Chomsky, 1988).

TABLE 2.1 The Language of Crime Wars

alert	drastic measures	peril
all-out attack	enemy	plague
armed forts	enveloping evil	potshots
arms race	feel the noose	punishment
attacking	fighting crime	put on brakes
battle	fighting the war	ROTC
battle cry	fights back	savages
battle strategies	firing line	scores
battling	flood	scourge
big guns	flood-tide	search & destroy
bloody	force	shoot
bombs	frontal assault	slaughter
boot camp	frontier	smashing
busting	front lines	stings
clamp down	fryers club	strikes back
confrontation	getting tough	striking
counterforce	harden hearts	struggle
crackdown	hardline	taking aim
crushing	invasion	target
curb	kills	trenches
curse	meltdown	up in arms
cuts off	menace	war
cutting	mission	war at home
dead on arrival	monsters	wimp
dead zones	new frontier	

Do the media merely reflect and report our culture of violence or do they help to create it? The newsweeklies, for example, construct for us a world and a society in which human nature inevitably leads us down the path of evil. Bad people cause crime, and only those who have learned to harness their urges—led by police and other officials who specialize in self-control —can fight against the evil individuals among us. But at best we can only hold the line against the inevitable evil within us. We must respond with the only language evil understands: force and sometimes war.

Our language can reveal aspects of our culture that we normally ignore. Analyzing our language of crime prevention shows how deeply seated is our war psychology. Reading even the headlines, much less the stories, of newsweekly crime coverage these last three decades reveals how violent and warlike we are. Consider the words and phrases in Table 2.1; they have been repeatedly used in such coverage.

Judging just from our language, much less our attendant behavior, what incentives do we give criminals to forsake their lives of crime and violence?

The media reproduce our violent language, reflecting the violence of official strategies and behavior. But the media also invent and embellish the language, searching for new ways to represent the violence upon which we so routinely rely (Rapping, 1991). With this bombardment, how could we expect the public to do anything but join in? In the resulting environment of violent responses, public opinion polls show people calling for blood—a charade of democracy paraded as only what the people want.

Wars—even if we entertain the possibility that they might be "just"—are inherently immoral and routinely counterproductive. Yet war is how we address crime. The lessons this teaches directly contradict those of a society that is truly free of crime. Such a society seeks peace, not war, and would pursue it using peaceful rather than warlike means. A peace movement against crime would reflect a significantly different culture, one dedicated to justice and human rights, the absence of which stimulates most crime and violence (Elias, 1993b). A society that takes victimization seriously is best equipped to take crime victims seriously. Such a society would not routinely promote war and then enlist the wounded in a new round of violence.

Officials know the psychological power of language, and they have taken steps to co-opt the language of peace even while continuing its wars. Police officers now routinely bear the title of "peace officers" even as they become progressively more violent. War making becomes "peace through strength" and offensive weapons are called "peacekeepers." Why do journalists—whose business is language—allow these perversions? When will the media find their own voices, their own language, and reveal the violent failures that our crime policies routinely turn out to be?

Crime Wars as Propaganda

Throughout history, once a ruling class has established its rule, the primary function of its cultural media has been the legitimation and maintenance of its authority.

George Gerbner and Larry Gross

Mainstream media coverage of crime and crime policy typically falls short of the watchdog function we expect in a democracy. Occasionally, the media ask the right questions about crime, implicitly challenging the status quo. They ask, for example, whether drug enforcement might be a threat to freedom, whether drugs should be legalized, and whether crime statistics might be pretty meaningless. Yet they routinely answer these kinds of questions with the conventional wisdom, thus providing the appearance of openness while actually promoting official perspectives. No, the newsweeklies tell us, drug enforcement does not threaten freedom, drugs should not be legalized, and FBI reports are good enough.

U.S. crime policy does not work. When officials try to convince us that it does, it is mere propaganda. Wars on crime and drugs do not succeed; when they are launched, officials know they will fail. Invariably, they have purposes other than curbing crime and drugs (Ericson, Baranek, & Chan, 1991; Humphries, 1981).

But officials only succeed in launching successive crime wars because they are not held accountable for past failures. The media—which provide our window on politics and government—let us down. By largely reproducing official perspectives, the media also disseminate propaganda (Carlisle, 1990). The media question crime policy only to tell us that if it is not succeeding, then it is only because we are not tough enough—not that the policy makes absolutely no sense ("Getting Tough," 1988). Abundant research now demonstrates the biases and distortions of the American media (Parenti, 1986; Solomon & Lee, 1991). Their amnesia alone robs us of our history and our ability to learn from past mistakes. As in Orwell's *1984*, our consciousness gets tossed down the memory hole, conveniently replaced by official stories. For crime, it dooms us to repeating prevention policies that do not work. Rather than promoting the public interest, the media act more to legitimate official authority, promoting far more social control than crime control (Cavender & Bond-Maupin, 1991; Schattenberg, 1981).

This profoundly affects both past and future victims. Most crime stories, such as the 35 years' worth of newsweekly reports reviewed herein, embody a tone and content that is sympathetic to victims. "Let's not forget the victim" is the endlessly repeated theme even while the victim is otherwise treated with condescension and paternalism, if not implicit blame and chastisement. Repeated doses of get-tough crime policies are promoted in the name of victims, even when they demonstrably do nothing to help or prevent victimization. Indeed, law-and-order policies arguably *increase* victimization by failing to address crime's fundamental sources and by intensifying the injustices that lie at the heart of most crime and violence. By not questioning these policies, the media collaborate in politically manipulating victims for ends that have nothing to do with reducing crime. The media abet victimization, showing not their concern for victims but rather their disdain.

Because the media take their lead from government, we should examine ~yes~ more closely how officials treat victims. What victim policies have been promoted in the last decade? How much have those policies really helped victims? Who controls the victims' movement that is credited for these policy advances? It is to these questions we now turn.

Note

1. In "Crime: A Conspiracy of Silence," (*Newsweek*, 1991), despite three decades of newsweekly preoccupation with black criminals, the author—under the theme of "rethinking" race and crime in the United States—writes that it is about time we broke the "silence" about black crime. If whites would admit their fear of blacks and if politicians and the media would say more about the pre- dominance of black lawbreaking, then it would—incredibly—get them to pay attention and respond to wretched inner-city conditions!

3

Victims

ALL DRESSED UP BUT NO PLACE TO GO?

> It is time to recognize the larger contours and consequences of develop-
> ments political scientists have long studied as fragments. . . . Laws and offi-
> cial actions that reassure or threaten without much warrant . . . are doubt-
> less conceived . . . as discrete events; but when, taken together, they reach
> a critical mass of complementary programs, they become an essential part
> of a new political pattern . . . that converts liberal and radical watchwords of
> the past into conservative bastions of the future.
>
> Murray Edelman

WHAT would we say about a movement that apparently forgot to invite most of its professed beneficiaries? What if we discovered, for example, in the victims' "movement," that victims were, politically, all dressed up but had no place to go? What kind of movement would it be? Would it really be a movement at all?

Reviewing recent victim policy makes these questions all too appropriate. The movement to redress the victim's plight has been much ballyhooed, but we must consider more closely what the movement and its resulting policies represent politically and what they actually achieve. Other than discussing

AUTHOR'S NOTE: This chapter is based on Elias, R. (1990). Which Victim Movement, in A. J. Lurigio, W. Skogan, & R. Davis (Eds.), *Victims of Crime* (pp. 226-251). Newbury Park, CA: Sage.

26

relatively trivial legislative "debates," the victims' movement has been presented mostly as if it had no politics at all. Instead, we should examine the movement's political evolution, particularly in the Reagan and Bush years, which have set the context for victim policy. We will emphasize "legislative" policy: the changes that have occurred, the new directions that have emerged, and the impact of the politics of the 1980s and early 1990s, especially those of the victims' movement.

Recent Legislative Policy

If we take the justice out of the criminal justice system we leave behind a system that only serves the criminal.
                                        President's Task Force on Victims of Crime

The victims' movement as legislative policy emerged in 1965 in California with the nation's first victim compensation program. Over the next decade and a half, national and state legislation steadily increased. Yet the legislative movement for victims was most successful in the 1980s, which saw a tremendous outpouring of initiatives. Mostly we are concerned here with American state and national laws, although international legislation also emerged during this period, casting the movement in a different light.

State Legislation

Most legislative activity has occurred in the states, providing victim services, changing the criminal process, emphasizing special groups, establishing victim rights, and dealing more harshly with offenders.[1]

Victim Services

These programs emphasize financial aid, logistical support, and personal treatment. Every state has laws bolstering the judiciary's common-law power to order restitution in money payments, transferred property, or work. Half the states mandate restitution for many crimes unless the judge explains in writing why it is not to be imposed in a particular case. Most states have authorized witness fees, some have raised their fee levels, and one pays lost wages. Thirty-five states reimburse rape victims for medical examinations.

All but six states have compensation programs. Most impose eligibility rules and pay for losses such as medical costs, psychological counseling, lost wages or support, funeral costs, and emergencies caused by violent crime. Some impose a hardship test, allow pain and suffering awards, and provide some property coverage. A few states support local nonprofit victim groups, compensate parents of missing children and dependents of firefighters and police officers, and pay child care or for lost homes.

All but two states have funded domestic violence services (for safe refuge, as well as for education, training, housing, and emergency medical, legal, and psychological support). Half the states fund sexual assault programs to meet victims' psychological and medical needs. Most states stress the victim's role in court: Thirty-four have created local victim and witness services to help victims exercise their rights, get timely information, and participate. A few states have special advocates programs.

Criminal Process

All states have laws to help the criminal process better serve victims' needs if not rights. All but two states allow a victim impact statement, which is an "objective" account (for the presentence report) of the injuries the offender caused; it is prepared by a probation officer or a victim advocate, or by victims themselves. Thirty-five states allow a victim to offer a statement of opinion (oral or written) about the appropriate sentence to the court. Many states have extended victim participation into other stages of the process, such as plea bargaining and parole hearings, and in the discharge, dispositional, mitigation, supervised, or early release hearings.

Most states require victims to receive certain kinds of information about services, their court case, and their apparent offenders. Laws require that police officers or hospital or compensation officials inform victims about compensation programs, and that prosecutors inform victims about witness fees. Other statutes require that victims be given notice of scheduled court proceedings, usually upon request; these include canceled hearing dates, pretrial release, bail hearings, plea agreements, sentencing, final dispositions, parole hearings, pardons, work release decisions, prisoner releases, and escapes.

Fifteen states allow victims to be in the courtroom at the judge's discretion (waiving sequestration rules), and one state makes court attendance a victim's right. Eighteen states mandate speedy trials, although with no set time limits. Some states limit excessive cross-examination of victims and plea bargaining (or increase victim influence over the outcome).

All but four states protect against intimidation and retaliation by toughening criminal penalties, specifying kinds of proscribed harassment, and allowing "protective orders." Several states have legislated against the long-term confiscation of recovered property, requiring officials to promptly examine its usefulness as evidence and allowing photographic substitutes. Other laws help victims by explaining to employers the importance of court appearances. Some states even make it a misdemeanor for an employer to discharge an employee who misses work to attend court.

Victims have been given privacy protection, such as that needed for psychological treatments following victimization. Twenty-two states protect victims' names and addresses, although only for sexual assault victims in some states. Twenty-three states protect child identities. Five have blanket protections for counselor-client confidentiality. Twenty provide protections for sexual assault counseling, and twenty-four have them for domestic violence counseling. Yet some states oppose privacy, claiming it impedes press freedom, public records access, maximum information, and victim assistance.

Some states have changed statutory wording, such as rape law reforms that reduce victims' burden of proof, broaden the proscribed conduct use language that is not specific in gender, and recognize degrees of force. Purportedly to better protect victims, other laws define new crimes, such as disclosing domestic violence shelter locations. Finally, 17 states require training in victims' issues for judges, prosecutors, and police officers.

Special Victims

Most states have passed laws for special groups of victims. Some emphasize child victims. All but nine try to make child testimony less traumatic, permitting a videotaped statement either alone (unsworn interrogatory) or under oath and cross-examination (deposition), or live testimony through closed-circuit television. Forty states have legislation about missing children, and many have created clearinghouses to help find them. More than half the states have amended child-competency or hearsay-admissibility rules, required child guardians, or extended the statute of limitations for child offenses. Somewhat fewer states require speedy trials or protect child privacy during prosecution.

Twenty-four states allow background checks of child workers, including access to criminal records. Nineteen states require everyone—and all states at least require professionals (such as licensed teachers, medical staff, and child care workers)—to report suspected child abuse or face civil damages or even criminal penalties. Some states have extended their adult bills of rights to children; 12 have children's bills of rights that require a guardian to tell the court the child's capabilities, the trial's likely impact on the child, when to use videotapes, and when to help with emotional problems and court proceedings. Children are sometimes given easier access to compensation and are exempted from testimony corroboration or grand juries.

Similar protections, such as services and shelters, have emerged for battered women. Better record keeping, such as monthly police reports, is required to track abuse patterns. Other laws provide protective orders, assign possession of a residence, require a defendant to pay support, and set custody and visitation rights. Thirty states authorize warrantless arrests for misdemeanor assaults; 10 require such arrests upon probable cause.

Sexual assault victims also receive special attention through laws that mandate services such as hotlines and counseling, crime prevention and prosecution, and medical attention. At least one state requires that sexual assault victims be given information about Acquired Immune Deficiency Syndrome, or AIDS. And changes have been made to reduce the victimization caused by traditional rape legislation.

Elderly victims have elicited laws that allow the victim's age to be used in determining sentences, which has produced tougher penalties and denials of probation. Some states criminalize the abuse or neglect of the elderly. Many states require elderly abuse reporting, especially by professionals, with 25 states protecting all vulnerable adults and 22 protecting older adults over a certain age. Some states mandate ombudsmen, speedy trials, abuser registries, hotlines, food, clothing, shelter, medical care, and other social services.

Other special victim groups have been added. More than 400 new laws related to drunk driving victims have emerged in recent years. Thirty-five states cover these victims for compensation, and all but one state has raised its drinking age to 21. "Dram shop" liability (for those serving intoxicated drivers) has been imposed by statute or case law in 42 states. Also, hate-violence victims have received some attention. Eighteen states criminalize acts that infringe on civil rights based on race, color, creed, religion, national origin, or sex; only one state protects sexual orientation. Thirty states criminalize the desecration of religious property, and 22 ban not only the disruption of religious gatherings, but also inappropriate hoods or masks. Forty-three states ban violence resulting from racial or religious hatred.

Victim Rights

Victim legislation has been increasingly packaged as statutory or constitutional rights. Since 1980, when the first victim bill of rights passed, 44 states have added similar laws, including the right to information, protection, transportation, property return, waiting areas in courtrooms, input, notification, employer and creditor intercession, speedy dispositions, and court attendance. Most states have passed formal bills of rights, but five have packaged existing legislation and four have passed legislative resolutions.

Because these bills provide statutory rights without real remedies for nonenforcement, some wonder whether these bills really provide rights at all. Some states encourage enforcement through an ombudsman or grievance procedure, yet officials are immunized against monetary damages for nonimplementation. A few states have adopted constitutional amendments to reinforce their bills of rights. They elevate statutory rights to constitutional rights; that is, they specify rights to dignity, respect, sensitivity, restitution, compensation, and to the opportunity to influence sentencing and be informed and present in the criminal process.

Offender Rights

By implication, some victim protections affect offender rights. Some initiatives specify that victims' rights shall not erode defendant's rights, but no specific provisions to ensure this are included. Indirectly, offenders' rights may be affected by victim participation in plea bargaining, sentencing, and parole decisions.

Directly, offenders' rights have been curbed by "notoriety for profits" laws, which confiscate profits generated when offenders sell their crime story, and domestic violence laws, which allow warrantless arrests. Restitution is now an enforceable civil judgment, and offenders are often banned from being considered crime victims themselves. Laws have weakened evidence rules for convicting defendants, eliminated the insanity plea (sometimes for "guilty but mentally ill" laws that impose prison terms preceded by assignment to a mental institution), and toughened (through "sentencing enhancement") criminal penalties (such as distinguishing felonies from "serious" felonies).

Courts have reduced the exclusionary rule's curb on illegally seized evidence, and legislation has done likewise. Many states have challenged the bail system by allowing preventive detention that jails suspects even if they meet normal bail-release standards and even without formal charges being filed. Only "tort reform," which limits corporate liability for victimization, provides laws that help offenders, although obviously not those who are stressed by standard law enforcement.

Funding

Victim programs have been funded less and less through general revenues: Only 16 states now do so. Some alternative sources are earmarked to fund particular programs, such as marriage license fees for domestic violence shelters; other sources are distributed more evenly.

Some resources come from offenders as a fixed or variable assessment for each crime; a criminal fine surcharge; a driver's license reinstatement fee; literary profits from crime stories; forfeited crime assets; recovered racketeering damages; and wages earned in prison, on work release, or while on parole. Other funds come from bail forfeitures or bondsman taxes, as well as from levies such as marriage, divorce, birth, and death surcharges; alcohol taxes; income-tax checkoffs; and court filing fees. Funding also comes from the national government in block grants and from the Victims of Crime Act.

Pending Proposals

Much more legislation awaits enactment, including proposals to reduce victim cross-examination, eliminate plea bargaining and the exclusionary rule, substitute affidavits for victim testimony, tighten bail requirements, require "truth in sentencing" standards from judges, and add constitutional amendments. Concerns about drunk driving, for example, have led to a campaign for increasing compensation, revoking drivers' licenses upon arrest, confiscating license plates, incarcerating repeat offenders, issuing color-coded drivers' licenses, and passing open-container laws. Legislation may also begin to address some neglected groups, such as rural or arson victims, and victimized members of "deviant" groups.

National Legislation

National legislation reflects the same concerns found in the states; indeed, it has stimulated many state laws. Yet Congress has also passed its own laws that affect victims both directly and indirectly.[2]

Direct Legislation

Although not actually law, the heyday of victim policy began in 1981 with the Reagan administration's declaration of National Victim Rights Week. In 1982, it established the President's Task Force on Victims of Crime, which soon provided a long list of recommendations, many of which have now been enacted or are being actively pursued.

In 1982, Congress passed the federal Victim and Witness Protection Act (VWPA) to promote victims in the criminal process, address their needs, and provide model legislation for the states. The act required victim impact statements, sanctioned (by criminal penalties and protection orders) victim and witness intimidation, mandated restitution (or written justification of why no restitution has been imposed), and tightened bail standards. It required the attorney general to set national guidelines for treating victims fairly in the criminal process, including services, notification, scheduling, consultation, accommodations, property return, employer notification, law-enforcement training, victim assistance, and crime-story profits. The guidelines were issued in 1983 but with the careful proviso that they were not enforceable as rights.

In 1984, Congress passed the Victims of Crime Act (VOCA) to provide direct national resources, through the Crime Victims Fund, to help finance state compensation programs, and public and private victim and witness assistance agencies. The fund had a cap of $100 million each year and was to be obtained entirely from criminal fines, penalty fees, forfeited bail bonds, and literary profits—and not from "innocent" taxpayers. The first VOCA funds were spent in 1986, with a fund limit increase to $110 million. In 1988, a new VOCA made a few changes, including directing states not to exclude victims of drunk driving or domestic violence, increasing the fund limit to $125 million and then to $150 million, and raising minimum-assistance grants per state.

Indirect Legislation

Some statutes have affected victims indirectly in omnibus programs, providing additional funding and easier procedures or imposing tougher offender treatment. Before the 1980s, some aid came indirectly from agencies such as the Law Enforcement Assistance Administration (LEAA); the Department of Health, Education, and Welfare (HEW); and the National Institutes of Mental Health (NIMH); as well as from federal crime legislation. The first general federal aid from indirect sources in the 1980s came in the Justice

Assistance Act of 1984, which provided block grants to states for improvements such as victim and witness assistance plans. That same year, Congress passed acts on bail and sentencing reform, which tightened laws against defendants to help victims, and urged states to do the same. The bail law allowed preventive detention, stiffened standards, and pushed the victim's role in bail decisions. The sentencing law restricted parole, limited judicial discretion, and mandated truth in sentencing.

In 1987, Congress passed the Criminal Fines Improvement Act, which was to track down past offenders and upgrade fines collection, partly to increase Crime Victim Fund resources. In 1988, the new Justice Assistance Act made child, spouse, and elderly victim programs eligible for new block-grant funding, provided some antidrug financing, and authorized funds to allow drug-crime victims to help law enforcement.

Special Victims

Since the 1970s, special victim groups have also been stressed on the national level. Child abuse laws began in 1974 with the Child Abuse Prevention and Treatment Act (CAPTA), which created the National Center for Child Abuse and Neglect (NCCAN) and funded public child-protection agencies, private treatment centers, and interagency cooperation projects. NCCAN helped stimulate child legislation in almost every state; in 1978 it began its first purported prevention program. In 1982, Congress passed the Missing Children's Act to address an apparent wave of child abductions. In the early 1980s, NCCAN's funding was slashed, but it was renewed again by 1985. In 1984, the original law was revised, emphasizing state treatment, identification, and prevention programs. In 1985, money from the Social Services Block Grant Act money not only went to training child-care service providers against child abuse, but also for health and protection for the next two years. In 1986, CAPTA first received VOCA money under the Children's Justice and Assistance Act, but those funds were cut significantly a year later.

Sexual assault laws emerged indirectly in the 1970s. The NIMH created the National Center for the Prevention and Control of Rape (NCPCR) and the Rape Prevention and Control Advisory Committee in 1976 to provide services, information, training, conferences, and technical aid—but no money for direct services. The LEAA funded some services but with nonfederal resources and almost never any feminist programs. LEAA programs emphasized victim cooperation and crime control, and its Stop Rape Crisis Center focused more on offenders than on victims. In 1980, some aid came from the Rape Services Support Bill of the Mental Health Systems Act, but by 1981 that funding was cut, NCPCR was gutted, LEAA was dismantled, and rape centers abandoned the feminist model and dwindled dramatically. From 1981 to 1987, rape center funding came from the Preventive Health and Health Services Block Grant of the Public Services Health Act, but by 1985 NCPCR had died.

Spouse abuse initiatives began in 1977 with LEAA's Family Violence Program, which in 1978 helped begin the National Coalition Against Domestic Violence, although it was reluctant to accept LEAA money and its restricted abuse model. In 1980, HEW began an Office on Domestic Violence, although it was eliminated in 1981, also the last year for funding from CETA, ACTION, and Housing and Urban Development (HUD) programs for battered women's shelters, programs that the Reagan administration mostly abandoned. In 1984, guidelines from the Attorney General's Task Force on Family Violence were released, and the Family Violence Prevention and Services Act funded prevention and other assistance, which was augmented later by VOCA funds.

Elderly victim protections began in the 1970s in LEAA and the Administration on Aging; these focused on security and education, not on direct aid. The Safe Streets Act of 1975 and the Community Crime Prevention Program of 1976 required states and then localities to propose new legislation for the elderly. In 1977, the National Elderly Victimization Prevention and Assistance Program emerged. By the mid-1980s, programs for the elderly still qualified for some general funds, but most had been completely cut several years earlier.

Other special victims have taken their place. Drunk driving victims have been championed in Washington and given prime attention in the 1988 Victims of Crime Act. Terrorist and torture victims have received some consideration. The Iranian hostage episode produced the Hostage Relief Act of 1980 and tax exclusions for government hostage victims. In 1986, the Omnibus Security and Antiterrorism Act provided monetary and nonmonetary aid for terrorist victims. In 1987, the Torture Victim Protection Act provided alien victims judicial relief in U.S. courts for past torture victimization.

Federalism

Federal districts and territories have passed some laws, but far fewer than most states. The Virgin Islands has victim compensation, and Puerto Rico has used some VOCA funding. The District of Columbia has laws for rape examinations, victim compensation, marital rape, hate violence, vulnerable adults, child abuse reporting, protection orders, restitution, victim privacy, and sexual assault funding, and it has proposed a victim's bill of rights.

Following the new federalism of the 1980s, national policy has emphasized decentralized victim programs at more local levels. Little has been carried out by national programs, which have instead provided guidelines, funding, and requirements for local practice, including priority for groups such as children, the elderly, and victims of sexual assault and domestic violence. National laws purportedly let the states set their own standards, yet many programs impose federal requirements anyway. VOCA funding for compensation has forced states to expand their medical coverage, maximum awards, and nonresident eligibilities and to reduce minimum awards or deductibles and limits on family violence and drunk driving claimants.

Pending Proposals

National initiatives have been numerous. The President's Task Force on Victims of Crime made 69 recommendations alone; others appear in the attorney general's reports on victim assistance and family violence, in funding legislation, in annual reports to Congress, and piecemeal through other means.

The national proposals now pending include victim access to parole hearings, family violence statutes, privacy provisions, dram shop laws, and reforms in sentencing, bail, and hearsay evidence. Most controversial are calls for preventive detention, more prisons, and capital punishment; limiting judicial sentencing discretion; admitting juvenile records into adult trials; an amendment to the U.S. Constitution; and completely eliminating parole, plea bargaining, and the exclusionary rule.

International Legislation

National and state laws are not the only ones that may affect U.S. victims. International or regional initiatives have addressed criminal victimization. The United Nations has passed such legislation, partly resembling and partly diverging from U.S. laws. International bodies have legislated even longer for victims to be defined more broadly.

Crime Victim Declarations

International and regional laws and standards have emerged since the late 1970s. The Fifth U.N. Congress on the Prevention of Crime and Treatment of Offenders (PCTO) stressed victimization's economic and social effects. In 1980, the Sixth U.N. Congress on PCTO addressed crime victims more directly (Lopez-Rey, 1985). By 1983, the Council of Europe passed a regional model titled the Convention on the Compensation of Victims of Violent Crimes (Willis, 1984). Crime victims were included in the model legislation of the U.N. Institute on the Prevention and Control of Crime, the International Law Association's Committee on International Criminal Law, and the International Association of Penal Law (Schaaf, 1986).

The United Nations' Sixth Congress was just as concerned with victims of the abuse of power, attributing to it far greater physical, psychological, and financial harm than common crime and calling for global action (United Nations Secretariat, 1980). The Seventh Session of the U.N. Committee on Crime Prevention and Control in 1982 repeated the call. In 1985, at the Seventh U.N. Congress on PCTO, acting on the World Society of Victimology's draft, the Declaration of Basic Principles of Justice for Victims of Crime and Abuses of Power was formally adopted and then ratified by the U.N. General Assembly (Fattah, 1992c; Lamborn, 1987a).

While a few nations, such as the United States, tried to limit the declaration to only victims in existing national criminal laws, almost all nations wanted (and got) broader definitions that encompassed both political victimization (such as through apartheid and disappearances) and economic victimization (such as by multinational corporations and national policies). The declaration covered both victim groups but provided more specific standards for crime victims, such as access to justice, fair treatment, restitution, compensation, and services. It invoked international law to reinforce its protections, urged strong legislation against abuses of power, and called for global cooperation to prevent both kinds of victimization (Fattah, 1989; Lamborn, 1987a).

Human Rights Declarations

The Declaration of Basic Principles of Justice and the preceding deliberations did more than consider different groups of victims simultaneously. It acknowledged relationships not widely accepted in the U.S. victims' movement, recognizing that far more victimization comes from governments and business institutions than from those defined as criminal under national laws, and that social victimization causes crime. The declaration was predicated on existing international criminal law and human rights covenants. The former includes at least 22 recognized crimes, incorporating international instruments that condemn crimes against peace, war crimes, crimes against humanity, genocide, slavery, hijacking, hostage taking, and torture. It encompasses the "collective victims" of crime and abuses of political and economic power, as reflected in the standards of the International Society of Criminology, the International Society of Social Defense, and the U.N. Economic and Social Council's International Penal and Penitentiary Foundation (Bassiouni, 1985; DeCataldo Neuberger, 1985).

As invoked in the Declaration of Basic Principles of Justice, international human rights encompass the U.N. Declaration on Human Rights; the International Covenants on Civil and Political Rights and on Economic, Social, and Cultural Rights; and the many specialized U.N. rights covenants on women, workers, torture victims, and others (Danielus, 1986). The declaration also incorporated the human rights protections of the U.N. Draft Code on Transnational Corporations (Lamborn, 1987a). It quite likely encompasses regional human rights protections—such as from Europe, North America, and South America—and even nongovernmental declarations such as the Algiers Universal Declaration of the Rights of Peoples (Falk, 1981) and the International Tribunal on Crimes Against Women (Russell & Van Den Ven, 1984).

Pending Proposals

Passing the 1985 U.N. Declaration of Basic Principles of Justice has shifted the context of victimization, at least in international discussions, toward a broader definition of *victim* that goes beyond criminal victimization; it has set a precedent for incorporating victims into international law and for an expanded concept of victimization, which will likely provoke more international and regional legislation (Geis, Chappell, & Agopian, 1985; Melup, 1991). It has already stimulated implementation proposals for a covenant to bind signatories (Lamborn, 1987a). The declaration may inspire national legislation, such as the proposed Canadian and International Charter of Rights for Crime Victims, which calls for protection, reparation, information, and treatment, as well as alternatives to the criminal process and to the social system that produces most injustice, conflict, and criminal victimization (Normandeau, 1983).

Evaluating Victim Policy

The system's failure is only in the eye of the victim; for those in control, it's a
roaring success!

Jeffrey Reiman

We can evaluate recent victim policy through research and political analysis. What does this legislation provide? How well has it been implemented?
What have its tangible and symbolic effects been? Has it helped victims?
Has it eroded offender rights? What does it reflect about the victims' movement? What is its political or ideological direction?

Program Implementation and Impact

The legislation reviewed above shows impressive victim activity in the
1980s. No wonder the period is viewed as a boon for victims. Indeed, these
laws translate into many programs and much new financing. For example,
between 1984 and 1986, nationwide victim compensation increased from $67
to $115 million (National Organization for Victim Assistance [NOVA], 1988).
Each year, the National Office of Crime Victims publishes an impressive list
of organizations funded by VOCA money (Office for Victims of Crime,
1988). Even some programs cut nationally have been resumed by state and
city governments (Smith & Freinkel, 1988). New funding mechanisms have
emerged, and rights have expanded. Some states have been especially innovative: California and Wisconsin with their bills of rights, and Michigan and
Florida for their constitutional amendments. Programs are providing help,
personally and in court, that would not otherwise be there (Maguire &
Pointing, 1988; Viano, 1989).

Problems

Nevertheless, when we look at its implementation and impact, victim policy
also has problems. Some advocates acknowledge what has been achieved,
but they claim that much more remains to be accomplished and that it is hap-
pening too slowly: Not enough victims' rights legislation and funding has been
provided, compensation restrictions remain, and victims' bills of rights need
enforcement (NOVA, 1988). Other advocates view laws as not the most effective victim policy (because the laws are often not actually implemented),

claiming that the courts should lead the way (Austern, 1987). Some worry that government may have promised more than it can deliver and that it has, for example, ignored information costs (Anderson & Woodward, 1985; Krasno, 1983). Others lament the fragmentation promoted by the "new federalism" (Smith & Freinkel, 1988).

More seriously, some advocates question officials' real concern for victims, wondering why services get such short commitments, why programs must be diluted to avoid administration vetoes, and why other programs are abandoned far short of solving the problem. One comprehensive study of federal victim legislation found it to be highly selective, underfunded, precarious, symptomatic, contradictory, and manipulative (Smith & Freinkel, 1988).

The state and local levels seem to fare no better. Consider the victim groups given priority in the 1980s. Some states have created trust funds, protective programs, and preventive services against child abuse, but they have been poorly funded and child victimization continues unabated (Morgan & Zedner, 1992). Sexual assault programs have increased in major hospitals but have dwindled in community health centers; independent centers have dropped drastically (Smith & Freinkel, 1988). Spouse abuse programs have survived (with diversified funding strategies) and even increased slightly in number, yet very unevenly, with a few states supporting most programs while others eliminate services (Smith & Freinkel, 1988).

Elderly programs, always limited anyway to crime avoidance, almost completely stopped when federal funding ended; far fewer local services exist than a decade ago, even though neither elderly needs nor elderly crime has been resolved (Smith & Freinkel, 1988). Restitution programs have been undermined by increased imprisonment and mandatory sentencing. Compensation programs have made more payments, but these serve only a tiny fraction of all victims.

Crime-control programs, enforcement crackdowns, and imprisonment have increased, yet crime has not declined (Elias, 1984, 1992a). Despite the policy, we have seen more victimization and more victims, especially women and minorities. For example, domestic violence is the largest cause of injuries to women in the United States, and it constitutes 20% of all emergency room visits. Three to four million women are beaten in their homes each year, and 1 of every 7 married women is the victim of marital rape. One quarter of all abused women are battered during pregnancy. One in four women will be sexually assaulted during their lifetime; 1 in 2 will be victimized by an attempted sexual assault. One in seven college-aged men admit that they have forced a woman to have sex; more than 50% claimed they would rape if they could get away with it. Hate crimes make up an increasing proportion of the violence against women (Wolfe, 1991). Serial murders have increased dramatically; men are the usual perpetrators, women are most of their victims (Faludi, 1991; French, 1992; Hutchings, 1988; Miedzian, 1991; Russell, 1986; Sedgwick, 1992; "U.N. Commission," 1991).

Likewise, minorities and especially African-Americans are the increasing and most likely victims of violent and other crime (Hutchinson, 1990b; Parker, 1991). Hate violence has escalated despite increasing legislation against it, victimizing not only blacks but also Asian-Americans, homosexuals, and religious minorities in alarming numbers (Clarke, 1991). When blacks seek redress for their victimization, they are less likely to be taken seriously than white victims, most of whom are also poorly served (Carter, 1988).

Blacks suffer, in particular, at the hands of the state. They are routinely victimized by police brutality: The Rodney King incident was hardly an aberration (Davis, 1988; Pearson, 1992; Reed, 1992). The warehousing of African-Americans in U.S. prisons (which hold more blacks than attend college) not only discriminates (Whitman, 1992) but also exposes blacks to victimization by and in prison (G. Anderson, 1988; Bronstein, 1991). Blacks commit fewer "index" crimes such as rape and murder, and yet their race and economic status guarantee their imprisonment in far higher proportions (Hutchinson, 1990b). The victimization of blacks is so systematic and so directly related to official neglect that we might well regard it as repression (Lawson, 1991). The violence of social and economic desperation has beaten down entire generations and communities, many of which are just waiting—like south-central Los Angeles—to explode (Jordan, 1992; Muwakkil, 1990). This is just the tip of the iceberg of the increasing violence of American society.

Administration

Problems with victim programs may stem from more than poor resources and meager commitments. Some obstacles may be organizational, caused by internal structural and ideological conflicts. The new federalism may be an impediment. Conflicts have arisen between traditional institutions and alternative centers, and between governmental and nongovernmental agencies, as the most appropriate sites for victim assistance.

Sometimes this is a matter of control; other times, it is professional ideology. Clashes emerge over using volunteers versus professionals, over independence versus institutionalization, and over philosophies of paternalism versus self-reliance. Conflicts arise among the law-enforcement, mental health, medical, social service, and other communities' perspectives found in victim programs (Smith & Freinkel, 1988). The problems do not end here: Victims have some of their worst administrative problems in the courts.

Victims in the Criminal Process

The victim's role in court has been much emphasized, producing many initiatives to improve treatment and participation. To implement them and help victims generally, dozens of victim and witness programs have emerged with the services outlined above. In sheer numbers, the initiatives are a success. Victim and witness programs have been helped especially by their recent federal funding priority. Many more victims now have help in negotiating the criminal process and the aftermath of victimization.

Misconceptions and Official Needs

Nevertheless, problems remain. Many legislative reforms for victims seem more symbolic than real. Despite marital rape reforms, for example, most victims still have no real recourse, and only one third of all prosecutions produce a conviction (Radford & Stanko, 1991). While new initiatives, such as sexual assault laws, have redefined rape and changed evidence rules, we see little sign that they have really helped most female victims in court (Allison, 1991; Estrich, 1987; Horney & Spohn, 1991; Messerschmidt, 1986; Sebold, 1989; Smart, 1989; Solomon, 1991). Other initiatives have been counterproductive: New antirape police units, for example, would seem to be a fine idea, but they have drained resources from highly effective, feminist rape crisis centers; undermined the feminist analysis of what causes this violence; and reduced the number of women assisted (because women are far less likely to go to the police) (Radford & Stanko, 1991).

Legal reforms against domestic violence have likewise largely failed (Ferraro, 1989; Henson, 1991; Hopkins, 1989; MacManus & Van Hightower, 1989; Reidinger, 1989; Sheptycki, 1991), and police officers still largely leave at-risk women on their own (Edwards, 1989). Accordingly, officials promote policies to keep strangers out of women's homes, and yet most violence that women experience comes from people they already know or who are already in their homes (Radford & Stanko, 1991). Like other services, victim and witness programs serve a relatively few victims, even though they are better funded. Even victims who have been assisted (by transportation, waiting areas, and notification), much less those who have not, often get victimized again in court primarily because of apparent misconceptions about what victims need and want and about how the courts typically work.

Policies assume that victims want to participate; that participating will satisfy their needs; that they fail to do so because of high costs, intimidation, insufficient rights and opportunities; that court personnel want victim participation; and that victim participation is necessary for effective criminal punishments. Yet these assumptions, made by victim advocates, policy makers, victimologists, and the influential presidential task force, may be wrong. Many victims have no big desire to participate and therefore shun opportunities to do so (Forer, 1980). A victim's testifying may not be a useful, cathartic experience, as argued, because the courtroom does not provide an appropriate setting (Henderson, 1985). Victims do not fail to cooperate because high costs, and victims are not needed (or sought) in most prosecutions; indeed, they are largely shunned as outsiders (Kelly, 1990). Victims may not participate partly because of unresponsive officials or because they realize it will not produce the outcomes or influence they want (Fattah, 1991).

More important, victims are irrelevant to how most cases are resolved: by plea bargaining in routinized, courtroom work groups, where victims jeopardize negotiations, slow proceedings, and threaten outcomes. Victim and witness programs may help promote dissatisfaction by treating victims as prosecution witnesses, thus building false hopes (Davis, 1983; Elias, 1990). Attempts have been made to curtail bargaining, but they will fail: Officials rely on it for workload efficiency and professional objectives. And eliminating pleas to get harsher convictions is unlikely to help victims because it is not necessarily what they really need or want (Henderson, 1985).

Ignoring Victims' Needs

Despite apparent victim concern, most officials still view crime as victimizing the state or society, not the victim. Some victim protections in court were devised for official needs and may not help victims, especially with their psychological needs. Indeed, they may be destructive and prevent victims from resolving their experience.[3] Victims can participate in sentencing, and yet such participation may satisfy no penal rationale or victim need.[4] Despite the many initiatives, victim frustration with the courts apparently continues ("Victim Rights Laws," 1987; Rubel, 1992). Participation may not be what victims want or need; nonparticipation or even noncooperation might be better (Elias, 1985b).

Rights and Punishments

Victim policy often assumes that defendants have too many rights, despite abundant contrary evidence (Rudovsky, 1988). Such policies emphasize a contest between victims' and offenders' rights; thus, most of the former have come at the expense of the latter (Karmen, 1984). Yet victims are poorly served by curbing defendants' rights; indeed, we are all losers by eroding our minimal procedural protections any further.

Some rights curbs are less important, such as banning literary profits from crime. Others are more serious: preventive detention, warrantless arrests, capital punishment, weakening evidence rules, and eliminating the exclusionary rule and the insanity defense. Other changes are also disturbing: mandatory and increased imprisonment, longer sentences, and eliminating parole—all in a nation already having the world's highest incarceration rate (Elvin, 1991; Mauer, 1991). These reforms seem to be a new dose of historically unsuccessful, get-tough policies that probably do little to satisfy victims' needs, which include not being victimized in the first place. Unleashing the state against criminals does not empower victims to pursue their interests (Karmen, 1984). Beyond offenders' rights, victim policy may also infringe on the rights of child workers, the media, and the public generally.

Some courts have found some victims' policies unacceptable, ruling victim impact statements to be unconstitutional in some capital cases (Sharman, 1988) and the Victim and Witness Protection Act as denying defendants' their Fifth, Seventh, and Fourteenth Amendment rights. Yet other courts have disagreed, letting victim policies stand (Kahn, 1982). Those policies have helped to produce and also resulted from a climate that has pushed courts further toward eroding offenders' rights by upholding capital punishment, preventive detention, and exclusionary rule limitations (Viano, 1987). The U.S. Supreme Court has led the way, adopting a criminal review model that equates rights only with those who are clearly law-abiding and almost presumes guilt and no rights for defendants (O'Neill, 1984).

Constitutional amendments may further affect defendants' rights, providing a presumption for victims' rights. They also seem poorly defined and hastily designed, have enormous yet unexamined effects on the U.S. legal process, have uncertain means for enforcement, and create rights conflicts with no apparent resolution (Lamborn, 1987b; "Perspectives on Proposals," 1987). They assume an adversarial process that rarely occurs and that may be ill-advised. They promote a "rights" approach to society, pitting groups against one another in a high-stakes, zero-sum game not likely to benefit victims, even if it is appropriate to favor them over defendants (Smart, 1989; Viano, 1987).

Politics of Victim Policy and the Victims' Movement

What political pattern does this reveal? We are concerned here not with narrow issues of how victim programs could be better funded or managed, or how they affect particular rights for victims, offenders, and others. Instead, we are concerned with what the victims' movement and policy represent as macropolitical phenomena. Why have victim initiatives emerged as they have, and whose interests do they serve?

Who Gets What?

Presumably, victims should benefit the most. Yet for all the new initiatives, victims have gotten far less than promised. Rights have often been unenforced or unenforceable, participation sporadic or ill-advised, services precarious and underfunded, victim needs unsatisfied if not further jeopardized, and victimization increased, if not in court, then certainly in the streets. Given the outpouring of victim attention in recent years, how could this happen, and who benefits instead?

Offenders have gained because victim policy has neither reduced nor even tried to reduce crime. But offenders have not gained when apprehended, because their rights have deteriorated and their prison sentences have increased. Victim advocates, including many devoted activists, may have gained from the emerging "victims industry," and yet overall the victim's loss is also their loss. That leaves only those who hold political power and who have devised contemporary victim policy: They have gained plenty.

It is hard to believe the apparent concern shown by politicians, not just because victim policy has achieved so little in practice, but because it probably could have been predicted to do so. So why pursue such policies? Perhaps because they provide other benefits, both political and ideological.

Ideological Stakes

Victim initiatives seem to perpetuate biased definitions of crime that are conveyed in legislation, enforcement patterns, or the media and that limit our concept of victimization to "street" crime, usually ignoring the much more harmful "suite" crime, be it corporate or governmental (Foraker-Thompson, 1988; Green & Berry, 1985; Woodiwiss, 1990). They further narrow those victims to whom we will devote our attention: not to lower-class minorities, who are among the most victimized, but rather to the elderly, children, and other victims who—however deplorable their victimization—are not among those who are *most* victimized (Parker, 1991).

Even these victims are often treated paternalistically as helpless and frail and thus robbed of any sense of power and self-reliance (Smith & Freinkel, 1988). They are designated, although not permanently, as the "innocent" victims we all want to protect; they may also be "safe" victims, who can help limit the movement—an apparent exercise in social control (Elias, 1990; Marx, 1983). With offenders, it is no different. The presidential task force narrows itself to a small array of common criminals; not those producing the most harm, portraying them and their supposed rights in mythical terms, and creating a biased view of crime and its sources (Henderson, 1985; President's Task Force on Victims of Crime, 1982).

Similar biases emerge in victims' programs. Consider federal victim services and the "issue definition" process therein. The extremes of victimization are emphasized, where the most horror can be raised but the least victimization occurs. Emphasis is put on protection, services, and education, but rarely on prevention; when emphasized, it is defined only in conservative terms, never examining crime's social sources and instead exhorting victims to change their behavior. Programs are treated as temporary, requiring annual lobbying for renewal, perhaps to avoid suspicions that the United States has fundamental social problems or needs any deep-seated "welfare" programs; indeed, much is made of how offenders rather than "innocent" taxpayers pay entirely for VOCA.

As for specific programs, spouse abuse is viewed as part of a "cycle of family violence" in "some" families and never as sexism in the broader society. Child "abuse" is regarded as the problem, even though child "neglect" is far more prevalent and damaging. Sexual abuse is viewed as a problem of lax enforcement and victim indiscretions, never as a problem of male society. The elderly are viewed as victimized mostly by crime, ignoring the greater victimization caused by the persistent poverty in which many of them live. Victimization's causes, when considered at all, never include such elements as class inequality, blocked opportunities, American cultural violence, or bankrupt concepts of family (Davis, 1988; Jankowski, 1992; Wright & Sheley, 1992). High-profile victims are shown apparent concern, and yet it emerges more rhetorically than substantively. Worse, the few resources made available for victim services come with "strings" that spread these ideologies far beyond Washington (Smith & Freinkel, 1988).

The elderly were "star" victims in the 1970s, as were their programs. Yet by the early 1980s, they were off the victim agenda, with their needs and victimization unabated. Like a passing fad, the victim torch seems to have passed to new "celebrities," who are likewise championed without much substance. Both victims of drunk drivers and abducted children have been the recent focus, even though research finds these victimizations to be exaggerated and politically exploited, more safe but dramatic victims whose stars will also soon fade (Eliasoph, 1986; Ellison, 1982; Walker, 1985).[5] Is this short-term attention simply innocent politics or the management of dissent with token programs that are used manipulatively until the fervor subsides (Piven & Cloward, 1971; Smith & Freinkel, 1988)?

Manipulating the Movement

No wonder that some critics believe that the victims' movement has been co-opted (Henderson, 1985; Viano, 1987; Smith & Freinkel, 1988). The victims' movement may be conservative and manipulated, it may be no movement at all, and it may be many movements of unequal influence, but it is hardly the politically neutral phenomenon that it is been portrayed. The movement we hear most about may not very well satisfy the definition of a social movement. The label *movement*, like *rights*, is often misapplied and overused.[6] A movement is a social or political phenomenon seeking fundamental change through mostly unconventional means (Garner, 1980). Yet the victims' movement we know has not fundamentally challenged U.S. society on its crime-control strategies, social policies, or otherwise.

Government has never been conceptualized as crime victims' main obstacle—offenders have; thus, the frequent alliance between victim advocates and government policy makers. If it ever was a movement, it ceased to be so when it became partners with government. This would be all right if government were really committed to helping victims and willing to admit its own contribution to victimization. It is not, however; so the movement may be coopted, an important revelation because the term *movement* has a powerful symbolic appeal, one that implies significant change; yet this change may not be occurring.

Aside from labels, how did the victims' movement arise? It was associated in the 1970s with liberal politics whose crime-control policies failed, thus ceding the field to conservatives who, in their law-and-order crusade, championed the victim's cause. Yet the liberal policy of rehabilitation failed because it was never seriously pursued; anyway, it is actually a conservative policy, designed not to question the society's performance but rather to help offenders accept it. An exaggeration of liberal and conservative differences often passes as "politics" in American society, perhaps diverting us from real politics and power. In fact, mainstream victim activity seems to be associated with conservative crime policies, even when liberals have held office (Ranish & Schicor, 1992).

In the 1980s and early 1990s a coalition of so-called strange bedfellows of liberals and conservatives produced the current victim policy, with the guidance of the Reagan and Bush administrations. This may not be so strange; it may merely be conventional American politics and not a real compromise of political perspectives but only a reiteration of conservative policies (Henderson, 1985; Wertheimer, 1991).[7] The movement may have been coopted not only by being diffused, but also by being "used" for reforms that may have little to do with victims. Yet it allows victims to be manipulated to enhance political legitimacy, government police powers, and an apparent agenda of further civil rights erosion; a symbolic use of politics to convert liberal rhetoric into thin air or conservative ends (Edelman, 1988; Friedrichs, 1983; Smith & Freinkel, 1988).

But it is misleading to view victim concern as a single movement; important strands exist beyond the conservatives and liberals (Elias, 1990). Some of the most useful initiatives have come from the "feminist" victims' movement, but have been undermined by the "official" victims' movement. An

"international" victims' movement, described above, presses for global initiatives and recognition of the relationship between criminal victimization
and abuses of governmental power. But Washington does not embrace that
movement's broader definition of victimization.[8] Neither does it take seriously
another victims' movement—the "human rights" movement—that considers
more than merely crime victims, and whose perspectives (except for those
who stress Soviet abuses) the Reagan and Bush administrations have roundly
condemned in favor of their international terrorism policy and a "new world
order."[9]

In 1981, the victims' movement got a national spokesman in Ronald Reagan,
who apparently launched the heyday of victim concern. Yet whether measured by the victims of political or economic abuses (of human rights) at home
and abroad, or the victims of an administration (and its successor) that was
itself committing more crimes than any previous administration, or the victims
of government crime policies that have been counterproductive to ending
victimization committed by others, the Reagan and Bush years seem highly
victim-conducive, if not victim-producing (Dorsen, 1984; Frappier, 1984;
Kinoy, 1988). These are the abuses of power (human rights violations) that
the international victims' movement has linked to the neglect, if not to the
source, of criminal victimization. Should we trust such a government to be
pursuing the best interests of even those victims it has recognized, or should
we acquiesce to the victims it has ignored?

The recent *NOVA Newsletter* may not have exaggerated when it said that
Congress, in renewing VOCA, was deciding which sectors of the victims'
movement it would be recognizing (Stein, 1988). We can probably predict
which victims' movements will continue being included and which will not.
U.S. administrations, whether liberal or conservative, seem willing neither
to examine crime's social sources (which a human rights analysis would
reveal) nor make the fundamental changes that would significantly reduce
victimization in the United States in the first place. Doing so would be the
product of a real victims' movement.

An Alternative Politics

The manipulation of victims for political gain may not have resulted from
purposeful intrigue; such manipulation may have been merely opportune as
the movement developed. Nor have victim advocates been ill-intentioned or

powerless in helping to shape victim policy. We are concerned here not with individual motives, but with institutional constraints. But no matter how we explain it, the adverse results are real enough. Is this the kind of victims' movement we want?

Indiscriminantly accepting financial aid and philosophical guidance from governments and groups who are most concerned with conservative crime policies risks co-optation and manipulation. Instead, we could pursue an alternative politics of building an independent domestic movement and practicing a new victimology of human rights (Elias, 1985a). Let us further examine the official victims' movement and how it may be manipulating worthy victim initiatives and marginalizing the competing victims' movements that embrace that alternative politics.

Notes

1. The following review of state legislation relies on Anderson and Woodard (1985), Henderson (1985), National Organization of Victim Assistance (1988), and Victims of Crime Resource Center (1988).

2. The following review of national legislation relies on Henderson (1985), Murray (1987), Office for Victims of Crime (1988), Smith and Freinkel (1988), Stein (1988), and Trotter (1987).

3. Preventive detention has been justified to make victims feel safe, and yet a victim's fear may come less from an offender and more from the shock of victimization. Incarcerating the accused has been advocated under the untested assumption that it will satisfy the victim's desire for justice. Speedy dispositions will resolve trials quickly but may not resolve the victimization—and probably make it even worse (Henderson, 1985, p. 976).

4. Victim involvement will not apparently enhance *deterrence*, and *incapacitation* relies on the offender's traits, not the victim's. Victims cannot help *rehabilitate*, except perhaps when related to the offender, where the victim perhaps should help implement but not determine the sentence. Victim participation for *retribution*, which relies on assessing blame, would raise as many questions about the victim's blameworthiness as the offender's. It also assumes that retaliation best satisfies victim anger; forgiveness may better promote psychological healing. Plea bargaining and mandatory incarceration render victim preferences for *restitution* irrelevant or futile (Henderson, 1985: pp. 1001-1010). No wonder that almost no victims use their right to provide victim impact statements (Villmoare & Neto, 1987).

5. The apparent concern for the elderly, women, and children comes from administrations that have massively cut social spending that might have spared these people victimization, both criminal and otherwise. And government policy has turned on the elderly, for example, in other ways: To shield them from financial victimization in their waning years, it has pushed "protective" plans that confiscate their resources and place them in custody (Gordon, 1986). Government has gone from viewing the elderly as victims to viewing them as a new criminal class, the same switch previously applied to women, despite the contrary evidence (Cullen, Wozniak, & Frank, 1985). How easy it is to manipulate groups: The elderly's main advocates promote the government's counterproductive, law-and-order crime policies. The government has also used ideologi-

cal screens in women's programs: Shelters and independent centers are totally out of favor and have been defunded—at least if they promote feminist goals of self-reliance and social change (Smith & Freinkel, 1988).

6. Here rights serve as a powerful rhetorical device to exploit public concerns about crime (Henderson, 1985, p. 952; see also Scheingold, 1974).

7. Nondecisions, or what is kept off the political agenda, are major power sources in the U.S. system, routinely excluding real alternatives from policy consideration (Smith & Freinkel, 1988). Also consider that the victims' movement relies on administrations that support (with few liberal objections) those who would force poor women to have unwanted children—to end "fetus victimization"—and yet once born, these humans are subjected to a lifetime of real victimization (Edelman, 1988; Kimmich, 1985). These administrations also label as victims Nazi criminals, Salvadoran death squads, Nicaraguan Contra "freedom fighters," and corrupt Arab sheiks; they also profess (still more) "wars on crime" while dismantling such enforcement mechanisms as antitrust laws, and they countenance (if not welcome) extensive corporate victimization, both criminal and otherwise (Green & Berry, 1985; Nader, 1986).

8. The United States was almost alone among nations at the United Nations in rejecting the connection between criminal victimization and the victimization caused by abuses of government power. Although the United States finally voted for a weaker version of the declaration, it has resisted its ratification, just as it has most other U.N. covenants (Frappier, 1984).

9. However, in pursuing torture and terrorism policy, the United States designates politically approved victims (convenient for ideological and foreign policy goals), while ignoring most of the rest (Chomsky, 1988).

4

Taking the Victims' Movement
for a Ride

The historical failure to pursue effective remedial action stems from a
pervasive contradiction. A problem to some is a benefit to others. . . . [Re-
sulting] policies reflect and rationalize the dominant pattern of ideologies.
In doing so they heighten the sense of dynamism the political spectacle
creates. . . . The most common course is the enactment of a law that
promises to solve or ameliorate the problem even if there is little likelihood it will accomplish its purpose. . . . [I]t is perennially effective in
achieving quiescence from the discontented and legitimation for the
regime . . . [such as] anticrime laws that have little impact upon the
frequency or incidence of crime.

Murray Edelman

Which Victims' Movement?

Driven by turmoil, political leaders proposed reforms that were in a sense
prefigured by institutional arrangements that already existed, that were
drawn from a repertoire provided by existing traditions. And an aroused
people responded by demanding simply what political leaders had said
they should have.

Frances Fox Piven and Richard A. Cloward

IN the 1980s and early 1990s, the victims' movement has finally flourished
with a wave of new attention, rights, and programs promoted by local groups
and governments and the federal government. Victims have been the appar-

ent beneficiaries of this new policy and activity. Yet we hear about the "victims' movement" as if it is a consolidated movement representing a broad array of victim interests and advocates. We rarely examine the movement's political perspective or direction; indeed, we act almost as if it has no politics at all.

In fact, the prevailing victims' movement has a very pronounced politics that has led it down a narrow policy path. Policy alternatives have been excluded just as certain victim perspectives and activists have been marginalized. As such, we can see not just one comprehensive victims' movement, but many of vastly differing power and prominence. The victims' movement we hear about has ridden the wave of recent American politics: It is a movement of political conservatism. Muted have been the victims' movements that challenge that conservative politics.

Thus the contemporary victims' movement is not as simple as it might seem. It has the possibility of uniting some "strange bedfellows;" more likely, however, it has merely excluded some members from the bed altogether. What is the prevailing victims' movement? Who leads, who participates, and what kind of politics and policy does it reflect? What are the competing victims' movements? Why have they been marginalized? What are their competing politics? In this light, must we question how much success the victims' movement has really had? Should we generate a new victims' movement to replace it?

The Official Victims' Movement

[C]oncessions . . . are usually part and parcel of measures to reintegrate the movement into normal political channels and to absorb its leaders into stable institutional roles.

Frances Fox Piven and Richard A. Cloward

Standard Definitions

We can delineate in various ways the victims and victimization we take seriously. The victimization we emphasize in our public policy and academic research should presumably include only significant harms produced systematically by individuals or institutions. Within that realm is a wide range of victimization to consider. But victim policy and victimology have mostly adopted the narrowest definitions of victimization: "criminal" victimization as outlined in criminal legislation.

A victims' movement has arisen around this narrow perspective, thus significantly reducing the victims and victimization it takes seriously. More important, the victims' movement accepts government definitions of the problem. Thus the movement responds to the direction set for it by government perspectives.

The prevailing victims' movement largely excludes everything not formally defined as crime, such as most corporate wrongdoing, even though it produces far more serious victimization than does common crime (Elias, 1990; Mokiber, 1988; Reiman, 1984). It marginalizes, except rhetorically, those harms defined as crime but which are not very seriously enforced, such as domestic violence, sexual assault, and white-collar and government crime. It encompasses some general categories of harm (such as that against children), but defines them narrowly in practice: child abuse rather than the larger victimization produced by child neglect (Smith & Freinkel, 1988). It recognizes the victims of terrorist acts committed by enemies but ignores the much greater victimization resulting from the repression practiced by its friends and by the U.S. government as well (Frappier, 1984; Goldstein, 1978; Herman, 1982).

Conventional Politics

Who constitutes the prevailing victims' movement? Largely, it is dominated by politically conservative organizations or groups that have been moved to support conservative policies (Carrington & Nicholson, 1984). A leading victim advocate, Lois Herrington, was appointed to chair the President's Task Force on Victims of Crime. Its final report, which closely adopted the administration's own conservative crime perspective, legitimized and then became a blueprint for the government's intensified, get-tough crime program. It uses an apparent concern for the victim to contrive a mythical view of a lenient criminal process and to fuel a dramatic rollback in defendant's rights and a vast extension of police power. Herrington was thereafter appointed as assistant U.S. attorney general in the Reagan administration.

The task force set the tone for victim policy and the victims' movement in the 1980s, producing a pronounced bias in which victim groups and perspectives have been recognized. Victim advocates holding feminist, antiracist, human rights, or anticorporate perspectives have been largely blocked from access to government programs. Instead, groups narrowly toeing the conservative crime-control line have emerged as dominant (Carrington, 1983; Gordon, 1990). They include organizations predicated on this line, such as the Victims Assistance Legal Organization (VALOR), the Washington Legal Foundation, the National Victims Organization, Americans for Effective Law Enforcement, California's Citizens for Law and Order, and Alabama's Victims of Crime and Leniency (VOCAL) (Smith, 1985). The meager attention paid to human rights victimization has emerged from groups such as Freedom House, which is devoted to an archconservative, procapitalist evaluation of violations.

Other groups, not inherently conservative, have nevertheless largely endorsed victim policies fueled by that perspective. For example, Mothers Against Drunk Drivers (MADD), Students Against Drunk Drivers (SADD), Parents of Murdered Children, and the American Association of Retired Persons (AARP) have vigorously promoted the antirights punishment model (Eliasoph, 1986; Reinarman, 1988; Smith & Freinkel, 1988).

Even more moderate victim-service organizations such as the National Organization for Victim Assistance (NOVA) and the Sunny von Bulow National Victim Advocacy Center have backed the conservative movement, perhaps biting their tongues in exchange for funding. The more progressive forces, such as the women's movement, which helped launch these kinds of service organizations, have been marginalized from victim policy (Young, 1989); what is left is a conservative core. This environment has also led once-independent groups such as the Guardian Angels, which provided some alternative to often heavy-handed law enforcement, to back reactionary initiatives: Consider the Angels' support for Bernhard Goetz, the so-called subway vigilante who illegitimately gunned down four black youths (Brady, 1981; Rubin, 1986).

Likewise, by largely accepting official definitions of crime and victimization, academic victimology, although perhaps populated more by moderates and liberals, has nevertheless embraced the conservative trend (Elias, 1985a; McShane & Williams, 1992). Even the American Civil Liberties Union (ACLU) has endorsed some victim legislation for fear that it will remain labeled as "antivictim."

If contemporary victim policy were likely to significantly help crime victims, then even with its narrow focus, perhaps the conservative tide would be worth supporting. Yet we must wonder how much victims have really benefitted, and if not, who has gained instead. We may have created much less of a victims' movement and much more of a "law-and-order" movement for other objectives (Karmen, 1984).

Predictable Policies

Even when considering only the legislation emerging in the last decade, the volume of victim policy is impressive. Many new rights and programs have emerged. New funding, especially from federal programs, has been significant, financing an array of victim groups. States and local governments have acted as well, producing new services, victims' bills of rights, and even constitutional amendments (NOVA, 1988).

State legislation has produced restitution and compensation programs, domestic violence and sexual assault programs, and victim and witness plans. It has promoted victim participation in the criminal process, better information, and better notifications. It has helped victims with protection orders, privacy provisions, and reduced cross-examination. It has reformed some criminal laws, such as rape legislation, and endorsed special training for law enforcers.

Several of these provisions have been elevated to "rights," some appearing together in victim bills of rights. The right to a victim impact statement at sentencing has been particularly emphasized. Most states have stressed special victim groups in particular, such as the elderly and victims of sexual assault and child and spouse abuse. Recent laws have focused on missing children and victims of drunk drivers (NOVA, 1988; Smith & Freinkel, 1988).

Just as important, much of the victim legislation has emphasized suspects and defendants' rights. Despite the occasional disclaimer, these laws assume that offenders' rights hurt victims; consequently, victims can be helped if offenders' rights are eroded. These laws allow warrantless arrests, weaken evidence rules, eliminate the insanity plea, dilute the exclusionary rule, endorse preventive detention, and significantly toughen criminal penalties (NOVA, 1988; Smith & Freinkel, 1988).

At the federal level, legislation has changed national policy and set the tone for victim initiatives at all levels. The 1982 Victim and Witness Protection Act encompassed the recommendations of the president's task force and provided model state legislation. The 1984 Victims of Crime Act helped finance state and local victim programs. The government has supported victims indirectly through other federal agencies and through laws such as the Justice Assistance, Bail Reform, and Sentencing Reform Acts of 1984 and the Criminal Fines Improvement Act of 1987.

The federal government has emphasized the same special victims' groups as the states and added two more: victims of terrorism and torture (NOVA, 1988;

Smith & Freinkel, 1988). And the government has gone even farther in eroding suspect's rights, either adopting or advocating such measures as eliminating parole, plea bargaining, and the exclusionary rule; more prisons and capital punishment; preventive detention; selective incapacitation; and an amendment to the U.S. Constitution (President's Task Force, 1982).

In sum, the last decade's victim policy has been impressive. Yet even without evaluating its actual impact for victims, we can recognize its narrow ideological bias. If the victims' movement has succeeded, then it has been in promoting a largely conservative crime policy that is designed to benefit a narrow array of victims.

The Hidden Victims' Movements

In each of these [successful] cases, people cease to conform to accustomed institutional roles; they withhold their accustomed cooperation, and by doing so, cause institutional disruptions.

Frances Fox Piven and Richard A. Cloward

Alternative Definitions

By definition, the prevailing victims' movement excludes many kinds of victims and victimizations, thus distinguishing those who are officially recognized from those who are not. Other victims' movements embrace what official recognition leaves out.

The more hidden victims' movements transcend official definitions of crime and victimization. They include corporate wrongdoing, such as environmental pollution and radiation, workplace hazards and disease, unsafe products and false advertising, adulterated food and drugs, unnecessary or incompetent medical practices, and product dumping, among others. These movements also take more seriously harms that have been defined as criminal but which have been poorly enforced, such as creation of monopolies and other corporate crimes, domestic violence and sexual assault, and white-collar and government crime. They respond broadly to human rights violations at home and abroad, not merely to the terrorism committed by selected enemies.

These marginalized victims' movements emphasize the more systematic victimization produced by persistent political, economic, and social problems. Thus, they address not merely particular crimes against women, minorities, and the poor, but also the victims of a more pervasive sexism, racism, and inequality. And they consider the victimization produced by domestic and foreign repression, which denies political, civil, economic, social, and cultural rights.

Although largely marginalized from the official victims' movement, this victimization has not been completely ignored. Although lacking the recognition and support of official government policy, it has attracted a considerable response from other victims' advocates and groups, producing alternative victims' movements that may better fit the definition of the word: They challenge and expand official definitions, shun conventional politics and institutional strategies, and pursue more fundamental changes in the American system.

Unconventional Politics

What are the more hidden victims' movements in American society? They include the feminist movement, the anticorporate movement, the antiracist movement, and the human rights movement. Their politics range from liberal to radical, advocating political reforms on the one hand and fundamental change on the other.

The Feminist Movement

The feminist movement, for example, ranges from the mainstream women's movement to radical feminism, and it emphasizes crimes against women and children: not merely those officially recognized or enforced as such (for example, sexual assault, child abuse, and spouse abuse), but also those produced by discrimination, poverty, prostitution, physical harassment, and other forms of sexism. Promoted by groups such as the National Organization of Women (NOW), Women Against Violence Against Women, and the National Coalition Against Sexual Assault, it challenges official solutions, advocates women's self-empowerment, and promotes an end to patriarchal institutions and society (Barak, 1986; Daly, 1989; Price & Sokoloff, 1982; Russell & Van den Ven, 1984; Snider, 1988).

The Anticorporate Movement

The anticorporate movement stresses the harms produced by the U.S. economic system and U.S. business. Led by groups such as the Center for Corporate

Responsibility, Public Citizen's Litigation Group, the Institute for Local Self-Reliance, the National Center for Economic Alternatives, the Citizen/Energy Labor Coalition, the Democratic Socialists of America, the International Association of Machinists, and the Infant Formula Action Coalition, it advocates redefining criminal law to encompass corporate wrongdoing, a serious enforcement system, and a fundamental transformation of corporate capitalism (Cullen, Maakestad, & Cavenderet, 1987; Katz, 1980).

This movement tries to prevent direct harms produced by corporate behavior and to eliminate the indirect victimization produced by the economic system. It advocates economic democracy to end several problems: poverty, inequality, labor and consumer victimization, community devastation, and economic exploitation (Frank, 1985; Green & Berry, 1985; Meyer, 1981; Nader, 1986).

The Antiracist Movement

The antiracist movement embodies a series of civil rights organizations, although, in part, it goes considerably further by envisioning the end of racism not through conventional political lobbying but through far more significant changes in U.S. political and economic institutions. Led by groups such as the National Association for the Advancement of Colored People (NAACP), the Congress of Racial Equality, and the Rainbow Coalition, the antiracist movement is concerned with political rights for minorities to prevent discrimination, improve political participation and access, and promote greater opportunity.

But eliminating official racism does not end unofficial racism as practiced by both individuals and governments. Thus, this movement addresses the racism that is deeply embedded in American society and which produces persistent discrimination and exploitation in the outcomes of the U.S. system: the marks of racism embodied in poverty and inequality, substandard education, inadequate shelter, nutrition and health care, dangerous and underpaid work, police brutality, criminal victimization, and official sanctions (including prison) that are applied disproportionally to minority lawbreaking (Dykes, 1983; Marable, 1983).

The International Human Rights Movement

The international human rights movement both encompasses and expands the victimization emphasized by the feminist, anticorporate, and antiracist movements. Although some of its advocates focus on smaller reforms, the broader movement stresses domestic rights violations including and exceeding those attributable to sexism, inequality, and racism. It is led by groups such as the National Lawyer's Guild, the ACLU, the Institute for Policy Studies, the Center for Constitutional Rights, the National Coalition Against Repressive Legislation, the American Friends Service Committee, and the Christic Institute.

This movement is concerned with the victimization produced by repressing political expression and participation, negating due process rights before and after imprisonment, using cruel and unusual punishments such as torture and capital punishment (or even prisons in general), depriving people's social and cultural lives, and denying a decent standard of living that includes decent work and adequate health care, education, nutrition, shelter, environment, income, and security. The movement promotes an end to repression and a redefinition of American rights, challenges conventional domestic and foreign policy, pushes for U.S. accountability within the international community, and seeks fundamental change in the American constitutional, political, and economic systems (Cooney & Michalowski, 1987).

These liberation movements emphasize a self-help approach to victimization, promoting more victim self-reliance than reliance on government programs. They also stress their connections to broader global movements: to international feminism, to movements for a new international economic order, to antiapartheid and other liberation movements in the developing world, and to antiinterventionist and transnational movements (DeCataldo Neuberger, 1985; Eide, 1986; Falk, 1987; Normandeau, 1983; Zalaquett, 1981). Thus we find them linked to international human rights organizations such as Oxfam, Amnesty International, Americas Watch, the International Commission of Jurists, and the World Council of Churches.

Also, while academic victimology emphasizes victimization by domestic crime, a significant minority has broadened its scholarly definitions and adopted more global perspectives: consider, for example, the World Society of Victimology's work for a U.N. declaration (Geis, Chappell, & Agopian, 1985; Lamborn, 1987a). These victimologists now join a growing number of academics who embrace feminism, economic democracy, black liberation, and global human rights. A more radical victimology could help the victims' movement avoid the narrowness and co-optation that it now suffers (Fattah, 1992b; McShane & Williams, 1992; Phipps, 1986).

Liberation movements focus on victimization as deprivations of rights, but they often also view these harms as crimes: They hold an expanding notion of "crimes against humanity" that equates rights violations with criminal victimization. These movements see a link between crime and sexism, inequality, racism, repression, and threats to peace (Pepinsky & Quinney, 1989). Likewise, they recognize the relationship between criminal victimization and the government's abuse of power. Taken together, these views constitute a dramatically different set of victim policy prescriptions, yet very few have been seriously considered by conventional U.S. politics.

Limits of the Victims' Movement

> It is not surprising that, taken together, these efforts [by the government] to conciliate and disarm usually lead to the demise of the protest movement, partly by transforming the movement itself, and partly by transforming the political climate which nourishes protest.
>
> Frances Fox Piven and Richard A. Cloward

The victims' movement's success may be more apparent than real. What are its limitations? How has it been constrained by its definition of victims and victimization, by its close association with official perspectives, and by the ineffective implementation of recent victim policy?

Myopia?

What does the victims' movement lose by accepting narrow definitions of victimization? First, it excludes other victimizations that result from systematic and significant harm. Why ignore or underemphasize victims of corporate and white-collar wrongdoing? Why exclude the victimization caused by racism, sexism, and inequality? Why marginalize government abuses that cause human rights victimization—if not for the questionable purpose of insulating officials from accountability? What kind of victims' movement would exclude these kinds of victimization?

Second, it accepts official definitions of the problem, the solution, and ultimately the movement. Even if blessed with the most benign government, this constitutes a poor if not naive strategy: Have the federal or state governments been seriously trying to end criminal or other victimization? Has any earlier movement against victimization succeeded by accepting the government's definition of appropriate policy? Or has the movement instead devised and pressed its own perspectives and policies upon an often recalcitrant government? And would a victims' movement not want to do this even more if our governments were not so benign after all? Short of severe pressure, has the U.S. government had a history of being concerned with victimization (Piven & Cloward, 1979; Zinn, 1984)?

Third, the victims' movement limits itself by isolating criminal victimization from other kinds of victimization. Such other forms can help us understand the effects of crime and why it continues unabated. Most kinds of victimization excluded from official definitions indict the U.S. system: They are accusations of repression, of human rights violations. They question the legitimacy of American society and institutions in their own right. These violations of political, economic, and social rights also describe the adverse conditions that provide the breeding ground for most crime and criminal victimization. We cannot easily separate crime from repression (Bassiouni, 1985; Elias, 1990; United Nations Secretariat, 1980).

Co-optation?

Beyond definitions, some critics wonder whether the victims' movement has been co-opted and whether it is actually a *movement*, which is defined as social or political action seeking fundamental change through mostly unconventional means (Garner, 1980). Yet the victims' movement has not fundamentally challenged U.S. society on crime-control strategies, social policy, or otherwise. Government has never been viewed as crime victims' main obstacle; offenders have. Thus, the frequent alliance between victims' advocates and official policy makers.

If it ever was a movement, it might have been co-opted for alternative government objectives: to promote more effective social control, legitimize government activities, and bolster conservative, law-and-order crime policies (Fattah, 1986; Henderson, 1985; Smith & Freinkel, 1988; Viano, 1987). If not this, then it is still an "official" victims' movement, almost entirely accepting government definitions, perspectives, and solutions (Morgan, 1981). Once institutionalized, a movement becomes depoliticized and limited to largely token gains (Radford & Stanko, 1991).

Ironically, by pursuing an official rights strategy, the victims' movement may have helped generate the backlash it now increasingly faces. By emphasizing rights rather than meaningful control and real power, the movement risks being marginalized as a cranky, special interest lobby. Embracing the *victim* label too strongly has allowed the movement to be portrayed as a bunch of weaklings (Lewin, 1992), complainers (Hamill, 1991), or even psychological dysfunctionals in the "recovery" movement (Haminer, 1992). Can we expect that the mainstream victims' movement, by shunning structural change, will soon suffer the same backlash now being experienced by the feminist and affirmative action movements (Faludi, 1991; Steele, 1992)? Some substantive change can come from legal or rights strategies, but we must also remember the formidable limits of using the mainstream law for social change, especially if it is administered by the same old elites (Neier, 1982; Scheingold, 1974; Smart, 1989).

The victims' movement never fundamentally questions official benevolence, thus ignoring the victimization that government itself helps to produce *indirectly* by pursuing historically ineffective crime-control strategies and *directly* by violating human rights, thus inflicting victimization and providing the conditions for the victimization practiced by others (that is, criminals).

Policy Constraints?

Besides questions of scope and control, the past decade's highly vaunted victim policies have had many problems in practice (Gibbons, 1988). Change has occurred very slowly. Victims' rights have been largely unenforced (Ellison, 1982; "Illusion of Victim Rights," 1989). Programs have been underfunded. Services have helped only a relatively few victims. Obstacles to qualifying for compensation and other direct assistance remain (NOVA, 1988). Although some programs have been added, many others have been forced to close, sometimes for ideological reasons (O'Sullivan, 1978; Smith & Freinkel, 1988).

Worse yet, victim groups such as the elderly and victims of child abuse, spouse abuse, and sexual assault have seen the limelight of victim policy only very briefly, with attention moving quickly to new "star" victims, such as missing children and the victims of drunk drivers (Elias, 1992b; Gusfield, 1981). Restitution has been undermined by increased imprisonment and mandatory sentencing. Competing professional ideologies and uneven commitments have placed victims in the middle of administrative conflicts among mental health, medical, social service, and other professionals (Smith & Freinkel, 1988).

Rather than being welcomed by criminal-justice officials, victims have largely been shunned as interferences to courthouse routines (Elias, 1990).

Legislative reforms such as new rape laws, which were ostensibly designed to help victims, have produced few changes for most victims (Beinen, 1981; Smart, 1989). Greater victim participation in the criminal process has been assumed to offer psychological and other benefits, yet it may do quite the contrary, producing instead increased conflict, stigma, dependency, frustration, and delayed healing (Fattah, 1986; Henderson, 1985; "Victim Rights Laws," 1987).

Conventional victim policy helps isolate the victims' movement from cross-national and international perspectives and initiatives: the United States, for example, has mostly opposed the U.N. Declaration of Basic Principles of Justice for Victims of Crime and Abuses of Power, rejecting the link between crime and repression. Victim policy constrains academic victimology, largely limiting it to conservative research and narrow alternatives. It also produces strange and unwarranted bedfellows, pushing the less ideological National Organization for Victim Assistance toward conservative objectives, and some radical feminists toward unnecessarily narrow and repressive (Ed Meese-inspired) solutions for problems such as pornography.

One study of federal victim policies, which have set the tone for all others, found them highly selective, precarious, symptomatic, contradictory, and manipulative (Smith & Freinkel, 1988). Perhaps most important, crime-control programs, enforcement crackdowns, and imprisonment have increased, and yet victimization has not declined (Elias, 1990).

In contrast, victim policy has been much more successful in achieving other objectives of questionable relevance to victims' interests. The policy has significantly rolled back rights protections for criminal suspects and defendants, a major blow to democracy with no demonstrable benefits for victims (O'Neill, 1984; Rudovsky, 1988). It has also fueled the rest of the conservative crime-control agenda, including new prison construction, increased incarceration, longer sentences, less parole, preventive detention, tightened bail restrictions, bolstered law-enforcement spending, drug-crime crusades, stepped-up capital punishment, and the continued demise of restitution, rehabilitation, and community corrections (Elias, 1992a).

This kind of "offender bashing" has not reduced crime or helped victims, but rather bolstered conservative state power and ideology and diverted us from the political, social, and economic sources of crime and victimization (Elias, 1990; Fattah, 1986; Reiman, 1984). Despite the benefits produced for some victims, contemporary victim policy might be more symbolic than substantive for most (Edelman, 1988; Elias, 1983). Besides the political manipulation of victims, the policy may constrict the victims' movement to very narrow expectations and policy options and prevent us from pursuing new and more productive alternatives (Bouza, 1989).

Toward a New Victims' Movement?

In these major ways protest movements are shaped by institutional conditions . . . . Yet within the boundaries created by these limitations, some latitude for purposive effort remains. Organizers and leaders choose to do one thing, or they choose to do another, and what they choose to do affects to some degree the course of the protest movement.

Frances Fox Piven and Richard A. Cloward

If the official victims' movement has limitations and perhaps even serious drawbacks, what alternatives could it pursue? We can outline here only some tentative directions, but presumably they would begin with strategies to broaden our definitions, avoid official co-optation, and pursue alternative victim policies. Movement organizers can develop for themselves a more independent path that is freer from government dominance and control. A new victims' movement would draw substantially from the more hidden victims' movements (feminist, anticorporate, antiracist, and human rights) without abandoning its interest in conventional crime victims.

Who are the victims who are marginalized along with our hidden victims' movements? To illustrate how official crime policy not only fails to serve crime victims but also creates new victims and victimization, we need look no farther than our most recent "war on drugs." It is to the drug war's victims that we now turn.

5

Wars on Drugs as Wars on Victims

Mama, Mama dey's a wolf at da door!
My Mama say, "What you come up here for?"
Mama, he say he come to save us from thugs,
He say he part of the gov'ments war on drugs.
My Mama say is you da same wolf what brought us to dese shores,
And destroyed our families; turned our sista's into whores?
Mama, he say yeah, but he ain't lik' he use ta be,
Now he really care 'bout us colored peoples and our family.
Mama, he say Nancy Reagan sent him to tell us: "jes' say no."
He say the gov'ment's truly concerned 'bout our welfare,
Mama say, "iz 'dat so?!"
My Mama say is you 'da same wolf what ran "Cointelpro"
And conspired to destroy Martin Lufa' King
wit' code name "Zorro"?
Yep Mama, he say he one-n-the-same
but everybody makes mistakes and everybody change.
The war on poverty left us mo' poor
and dependent on crumbs from you
So jes' what is dis "war on drugs" 'sposed to do?

Kenneth Carroll, "Wolf's at the Door"

Drug Wars for Whom?

PEOPLE have good reason to wonder about the U.S. war on drugs. Our memories are short, yet our current antidrug crusade has a familiar ring. Have we not fought these wars before? Did we not use the same strategies? Why does the problem seem worse than ever?

We have pursued these wars before. Early this century, we fought alcohol. When Prohibition failed, we pursued, in successive "wars," other drugs, such as opium, heroin, marijuana, LSD, and now cocaine. We have lost all of these wars; we will lose this one, too. Although they have not eradicated drugs, our wars have achieved other goals, however dubious; perhaps that is why they are launched in the first place.

Typically, our current crusade emphasizes a military and enforcement model. It uses criminalization, firepower, intervention, and punishment rather than decriminalization, treatment, education, and social change. Drug wars do not reduce crime, drug use, or the social diseases that cause them; instead, they increase victimization. Although painful to admit, our drug policies are less wars against drugs and more wars against victims and political change.

What drives our drug wars down this path? What victimization do they produce? What do they really achieve? What alternatives could we pursue?

Drug Wars as Propaganda Wars

Symbolic Crusade

Truth is the first victim of war. Media and government propaganda distort the drug problem and its sources, selling the American public on one drug crusade after another (Carlisle, 1990). Propaganda manipulates symbols to generate public support and sacrifice (Gusfield, 1981). We pursue "wars" and not merely drug policies, thus justifying any tactic to meet the threat (Rabine, 1989).

We have seen the "Vietnamization" of our drug wars. We "dehumanize" the "enemy" and can no longer distinguish "crack" cocaine dealers from crack users from crack neighborhoods from inner cities generally. Simply by where they live, people are assumed to be collaborators. Neighborhoods become "free-fire zones." We stress "body counts" and "firepower," periodically "widening the war," adding new targets at home and abroad. We trap ourselves in a quagmire: We are losing the war and yet cannot admit defeat, so we recommit ourselves to a hopeless objective. Eventually, we will pull out, after thousands of unnecessary casualties, claiming we have won (Brauer, 1990; Wenner, 1990).

Government Propaganda

In selling U.S. drug wars, the federal government—particularly the executive branch—leads the way, manipulating public opinion, whipping up support for official drug policy. It announces each new drug war and ignores our many similar but failed campaigns in the past (Epstein, 1977; Herman, 1989; Regush, 1971; ya Salaam, 1988).

Officials reassure us we are winning the war. Yet while the numbers of enforcement police agents have doubled since 1980, drugs have steadily increased. Drug volume has grown by 1,750% since 1970, tripling between 1980 and 1985, and doubling again between 1989 and 1990 (Blair, 1990; Knoll, 1989). Cocaine use quadrupled in the Reagan years (Miller, 1990). Determined dealers develop new drugs such as crack cocaine to circumvent enforcement (Shannon, 1988). Border interdiction stops only some 10% of the drug flow—and always only temporarily (Schmoke, 1989).

Officials claim that harsh enforcement and punishments are the only answer. Former drug "czar" William Bennett even advocates beheading for dealers: He should consider Iran's escalating drug use despite its summary executions of 179 drug dealers in 2 years (Trebach, 1990). Drug wars produce a chilling cost-benefit ratio: Unchecked drug abuse costs a fraction of the $80 billion we spend yearly on enforcement. Meanwhile, the government slashes resources from housing, welfare, nutrition, and child services (Nadelmann, 1988). Ronald Reagan left office proclaiming victory in the drug war; a year later, George Bush called the drug problem unprecedented and relaunched the same old strategies (Treaster, 1992).

Officials use drugs as the scapegoat for school dropouts, crumbling infrastructure, declining child services and job training, increasing violence, uncontrolled budgets and debts, police brutality, poverty and inequality, poor health, decreasing minority life expectancies, hate crimes, illiteracy, and homelessness (T. Williams, 1990). Officials promote double standards and focus on lower-class minority members, drug users, and small dealers rather than on upper-class whites, money launderers, and big dealers (Gould, 1990; Hoffman, 1987). African-Americans are the enemy even though whites use and deal far more drugs (Knoll, 1989).

Officials decry illegal narcotics and yet tolerate far more lethal drugs, which are relentlessly pushed on minorities, young women, and working-class whites. Approximately 3,000 people die annually from illegal drugs, while 500,000 die from alcohol and nicotine and at a net yearly cost of $52 billion (White, 1988). The drug war does not prevent Washington from subsidizing the tobacco industry's "new opium wars," which push cigarettes on children in Asia (Ridgeway, 1989). Officials feign interest in drug treatment and education, and then allocate 95% of their budgets to enforcement. Treatment means a prison term with no rehabilitative programs (King, 1989). Funding for jailhouse treatment has been eliminated, and successful prison programs, such as New York City's Stayin' Out, have been cut (Corn, 1990).

Officials exaggerate drug addiction's impact, ensuring sufficient hysteria to support its policies. Drug abuse can devastate addicts, their friends, and their families, but most illegal drugs do not produce instant addiction or high health risks (Martz, 1990), nor does use equal abuse (Goldstein, 1988). Approximately 22 million Americans have used cocaine, but only a tiny portion have used it in crack form. Only 1 in 22 are regular users (once a week, or more) (Levine & Reinarman, 1987). Officials describe addiction as a chemical or genetic disease, conveniently abdicating responsibility, when it actually is a social or psychological disease that is caused by adverse environments that officials help to create (Willis, 1989).

Officials generate significant new crimes by criminalizing drugs, and yet they blame the drugs themselves for crime. Or worse: White House adviser Carlton Turner claims marijuana causes homosexuality (Levine & Reinarman, 1987). We are back to *Reefer Madness* scare tactics, the propaganda that launches all of our drug wars.

Media Propaganda

Rather than a watchdog that scrutinizes government drug wars, the mainstream media reproduce official propaganda: the drug problem, stripped of its social context, can only be solved by harsh enforcement (Brownstein, 1991). The media bury U.S. drug history: The drug wars we have already fought and lost, one shady drug czar after another, presidential commission recommendations to decriminalize, and our long national history of habits (Corn, Gravley, & Morley, 1989; Goldstein, 1988; Petit, 1988). The media promote drug hysteria, which may affect the mind and common sense more than the drugs themselves (Gitlin, 1989): Incredibly, *Reader's Digest* reports, "From Middle America Come Reports of Teen Parties Where Cocaine Is Sprinkled on the Popcorn." Like drug addiction, the threshhold for satisfying our drug-control frenzy keeps rising (Ehrenreich, 1989).

The media perpetuate drug war hypocrisy. They ignore the government's own drug involvement: CIA profiteering in Southeast Asia, propping up repressive dictators, financing counterrevolutions, drugging prisoners, pushing alcohol and tobacco abroad, and CIA director and then Vice President George Bush's sponsorship of Manuel Noriega (Hinckle, 1990; Kruger, 1980;

Kwitny, 1987; McCoy, 1984; Morley, 1988; Other Americas Radio, 1990a, 1990b). The media ignored Bush's staged Lafayette Park drug bust, which dramatically launched his drug war to unsuspecting Americans. They have placidly promoted Nancy Reagan's futile "Just Say No" campaign in inner cities: Even though minorities cannot "just say no" to rampant poverty and unemployment (Katz, 1990; Rabine, 1989).

Media and government voices on drug policy converge, blurring press independence and fact and fiction. *Drug Wars*, a fictional television drama loosely incorporating former Drug Enforcement Administration (DEA) agent Kiki Camarena's death, was treated as fact by NBC's news division despite its endless distortions. The movie, using the DEA as consultant, blamed the drug problem on Mexico, justifying U.S. intervention as the only option. In successive postmovie interviews, NBC News anchor Tom Brokaw drew exactly the same conclusions. The White House scripted both the movie and the news (Massing, 1990).

The media and the advertising industry, which created our "culture of addiction," now campaign against illegal drugs with dozens of commercials, peddling the drug war to American consumers just as they would another box of soap. To dramatize drugs' dangers, we see sweating rats, eggs sizzling in a frying pan, coke-snorting schoolbus drivers, and girls jumping into empty swimming pools ("War by Other Means," 1990a). Psychologists tell us that these ads are likely to stimulate as much drug use as they stop (Levine & Reinarman, 1987). The ads also lie: The distorted brain waves of a marijuana user in one ad were really those of a mentally handicapped person (Savan, 1989).

The Partnership for a Drug Free America—comprising 75 top ad agencies—condemns illegal narcotics, telling us, "Drugs are perceived to make you feel good or powerful, make you less inhibited socially, make your sex life better, give you extra energy, and make you more popular." Yet the industry has used this same pitch to sell us products from cars to deodorants for 50 years. These same agencies use these appeals to target liquor, beer, and cigarette ads to Latinos, African-Americans, and women (Cotts, 1992).

Time says that legalizing drugs would send a "message of unrestricted hedonism," yet we get just that each day when we watch radio or television, cruise a shopping mall, or glance at a billboard. Structurally, we already live in a drugged society, massively ingesting legal narcotics, compulsively buying and consuming, riding fast cars, living fast lives, and searching for new highs. The biggest U.S. pusher is our consumer culture (Ehrenreich, 1989), which has primed us for drug abuse (Savan, 1989; Viano, 1990).

Motion pictures exploit our drug fears: Rambos and Terminators have now switched from the Soviets to the drug lords to wreak their vengeance (McConahay & Kirk, 1989). In the music business, sanctimonious appeals by rock stars provide little help. Predictably, a recent Grammy Award went to Bobby McFerrin for his carefree "Don't Worry, Be Happy," over Tracy Chapman's "Talkin' 'Bout a Revolution," which indicts the social ills that breed problems such as drug abuse.

Drug War Victims

Contrary to the propaganda, drug wars increase victimization. Our liberties decline, while our policies victimize the poor, minorities, the ill, women, children, drug users and suspects, foreigners, and even police officers. Drug wars increase both the victims of crime and injustice generally.

Liberties as Victims

Ronald Reagan launched his drug crusade as "another war for our freedom," yet in practice we are told we must pay for drug control with fewer freedoms. But while our liberties decline, drugs flourish. Not just defendants suffer: We all do. At least 11 federal and countless state and local agencies now fight the drug war ("It Doesn't Have To Be Like This," 1989). They are empowered to eavesdrop, to spy, and to monitor. They exploit the so-called "drug exception to the Fourth Amendment" (Navasky, 1990), which negates the exclusionary rule, and allows warrantless searches, stops and frisks, roadblocks, and privacy invasions (Davis, 1988). Police use neighborhood informants, identification checks to enter one's home, auto confiscations, armored cars, battering rams, computer files, and extensive new armaments—all of which bring increased brutality and violence. This produces the entrapment not just of individuals but also of entire communities (Levine, 1990; Wisotsky, 1986).

Courts order evictions, preventive detention, shock incarceration, illegal extraditions, and subpoenas that force attorneys to inform on their clients. Children are applauded for turning in their parents. Anyone remotely associated with drugs is stigmatized and isolated. The military assumes civilian functions. These are ingredients for a police state, for a "Big Brother" to watch over us (Baum, 1992; Rabine, 1991; Spence, 1988; Trebach, 1990).

Witch Hunts

The drug war resembles a McCarthy-like witch hunt (Wenner, 1990). Former drug czar Bennett dismantled federal aid to schools and the humanities. Continuing his call for a "return to authority," his policies indeed seem authoritarian (Zimring & Hawkins, 1989). Bennett, who is addicted to three packs of cigarettes per day and who spent his college days turning in student pot users, parades as a moral crusader, pitting the good guys against the bad and pushing punishment and force as the only answers (Ivans, 1990).

Washington, DC, showcased his get-tough drug policy, producing security fences and armed guards around housing projects, mass police sweeps of ghetto streets, neighborhood quarantines, identification cards and computer registration (shades of South Africa) for minorities, martial law curfews for inner-city youths, wholesale family evictions for suspected drug use, and roundups for Potomac River prison barges. This affects few drug dealers; instead it targets the drug problem's victims (Wenz, 1989).

Rather than politicians and the media challenging these injustices, they instead endorse them. Being "soft on drugs" is like being "soft on communism." Drug crusades produce political mileage; doubters are "drug-baited" as people who must favor drugs (Levine & Reinarman, 1987). The repressive Omnibus Drug Law of 1988 received overwhelming congressional support despite defining addiction as a crime, providing mandatory and lengthy punishments (including the death penalty), and directing 95% of its appropriations to police operations (Wenz, 1989).

How has this power been used? Teams of federal agents carried out 300 Washington evictions in one week that were targeted from government-sponsored housing blacklists. A recent Los Angeles ghetto sweep arrested 1,500 people in one evening, confiscated 200 cars, and yielded only $3.20 cash per person and just 19 ounces of marijuana and 8 ounces of cocaine. Imagine what a similar sweep would produce in a suburban white neighborhood? A far bigger haul and an enraged outcry.

Drug courier profiles produce groundless searches of African-Americans and other minorities. Wrong-address raids wreck homes, costing thousands of dollars. Secondary crimes, generated by drug criminalization, flourish, including assaults, murders, robberies, tax evasion, money laundering, bribery, and kidnapping. Government corruption grows locally and federally, as in the Iran-Contra scandal.

Drug wars violate international law, whether they be Colombian extraditions, Mexican incursions, or the U.S. invasion of Panama (Morganthau, 1990). The federal government launched its Campaign Against Marijuana Planting (CAMP) program in the mid-1980s, ditching the Fourth Amendment and deploying U-2 spy planes and helicopters. Partly funded by Budweiser beer, CAMP increased prices, police violence, chemical poisoning, indoor growing, and, ultimately, the yield, producing triple the annual harvests and far more pot for sale (Strickman, 1990; Witkin & Cuneo, 1990).

Bladder Patrols

When asked if he favored mandatory drug testing for athletes, former major league pitcher Bill Lee replied, "Well, I've tried pretty much all of them [drugs], but I'm not sure I'd want to make it mandatory." Obviously, this is not what officials have in mind. Instead, the U.S. Supreme Court has allowed routine, even mandatory, drug testing despite Fourth Amendment and other objections. Laws such as the Drug Free Workplace Act of 1988 mandate testing not only for federal and state employees, but also for millions working for private firms, including half of the *Fortune* 500 companies (Levine & Reinarman, 1987). The tests typically exclude alcohol, nicotine, caffeine, steroids, and prescription drugs—even though these substances are more dangerous than those being screened (Navasky, 1990).

These tests judge people by what they do off the job, not on. Justified to ensure employee alertness and consumer safety, the tests ignore more serious but legal drugs and the consequences of employee stress, long hours, and bad conditions. Officials scapegoat drugs for declining U.S. productivity even though business journals blame capital flight, excessive mergers, and poor management. Things such as parenting, fatty foods, and love affairs might affect work performance; will employers and governments regulate them, too?

Urine tests produce thousands of false positive findings (Levine & Reinarman, 1987). Even when accurate, they cannot tell what if any impairment results. Those who refuse tests are presumed guilty, which leads many people to be fired or not hired (Hentoff, 1986). Is the urine test the 1980s version of the 1950s loyalty oath (Willis, 1989)? When not fired outright, employees are put in authoritarian programs that use "breakdown therapy" and intimidation. Enforcement, not treatment, prevails: So-called "bladder cops" infringe liberties almost at will (Hoffman, 1990). But who and what get tested the most? Does such testing reintroduce job discrimination under another guise? Urinalysis now weeds out more than drugs users: Testing is done to establish pregnancy, HIV infection (and the suspicion of homosexuality), cholesterol, and even genetics (Navasky, 1990).

Students, especially athletes, also are widely tested. Chicago's St. Sabina elementary school, for example, has a random urinalysis program (Morganthau, 1990). Schools in Hawkins, Texas, spend $22 per student on drug testing, four times what they spend on library books (Levine & Reinarman, 1987). Searches and seizures of student lockers have been upheld. Some grade school teachers must be tested to get tenure. Researchers must take antidrug oaths to receive federal grants. Low-income college students lose financial aid if they are not tested (Grube, 1990).

We sacrifice rights through ruthless enforcement and by criminalizing drug use in the first place. As a victimless crime, it hardly justifies the government's forceful intrusion into our lives (Richards, 1982). More ominously, labeling the drug war an "emergency" has legitimized repressive tactics. Will it be a precedent for ever more emergencies and thus permanent rights rollbacks (Willis, 1989)?

Poor and Minorities as Victims

Drug wars promote official abuses of power. We all suffer, but poor and minority communities are especially victimized.

The Elusive American Dream

In poor and minority communities, most drug abuse comes not from individuals, who are labeled by official drug policy as either "weak" or "evil," but rather from their social context. Drugs reflect failures in the American dream: social ills such as unemployment, urban blight, malnutrition, illiteracy, homelessness, disease, and inadequate economic opportunities (Dykes, 1983; Kasarda, 1990; Marable, 1983).

In response, some users spend scarce resources on drugs to escape boredom, frustration, and the contradiction between their lives and the affluent society (Great Atlantic Radio, 1990) or to maintain the illusion of the American dream (Blair, 1990). For others, drugs make them part of a "culture of refusal" that rejects the system that has rejected them. Either way, this can produce not only addiction, but also AIDS, hepatitis, and other health problems. People are victimized by their environment when a high drug supply tempts and then hooks them, and they have no alternatives or treatment possibilities; instead they are pursued as criminals. We see this described as "black pathology," with whites as the victims. Yet the real pathology may lie in American society, with minorities as the primary victims (Reed, 1989).

For other users, drugs provide their only apparent chance of achieving the American dream. Minorities want what the United States promises: power, wealth, respect, and prestige. Given few options to make good, illegitimate means are tempting, and not just in the ghetto: Some family farmers, devastated by U.S. farm policies, now illegally cultivate marijuana to survive (Ridgeway, 1989). Capitalism teaches people to pursue the best opportunities. The legal system tolerates high-level economic lawbreaking; why should smaller capitalists be any different (Chambliss, 1989; Hutchinson, 1989)?

Enforcement as Social Control

Drug enforcement in poor communities does not reduce crime, violence, or drug abuse. Instead, it escalates it, rationalizing intensified police operations that seem more concerned with social control than crime control. African-Americans suffer enormous violence: The structural violence of poverty has reduced black life expectancy. And murder kills more young black men than anything else (Morganthau, 1989), and most murders are drug-related. Washington, DC, averages 10 murders each week; 90% involve drugs (Morley, 1988; Tidwell, 1989). Former Mayor Marion Barry once said, "Outside of the killings, we have one of the lowest crime rates in the country." Too bad that killings count as crime; how many fewer would we have without drug criminalization?

Criminalization makes the drug trade profitable but risky. Violence escalates to settle high-stakes disputes or to support one's habit (Lazere, 1990b). Police violence increases accordingly. A cycle of violence imprisons people at home, as they keep off streets that are taken over by drug wars. Police raids close down one neighborhood, but only push the violence on to others (T. Williams, 1990).

Officials systematically refuse to alleviate the drug trade's underlying social sources (Vergara, 1990). Criminalization and enforcement are counterproductive, and yet they are repeatedly pursued: Thus, they must be serving some other objective. Antidrug crusades have been conducted historically to control immigrants, minorities, and other repressed groups (Duster, 1970; Musto, 1973; Parato, 1990; Reinarman, 1988). Current drug wars continue that tradition.

Drug enforcement has helped to shape the brutality and double standards of policing African-American communities (Williams & Murphy, 1990). Officials discriminate in defining drug crime and drug profiles, arrests, and punishments. Whites account for 80% of illegal drug use, and yet minorities constitute 80% of those arrested (Johnson, 1990). Middle- and upper-class cocaine use draws lax enforcement, while lower-class crack use has launched a full-scale war (Glasser & Siegel, 1991).

Get-tough enforcement does not curb drugs, but it does help control "troublesome" populations (Bridges & Fekete, 1985; Cohen, 1985; Hutchinson, 1990a). In the ghetto, "Just Say No" translates into "Just Do As You're Told" (Lazere, 1990b). In earlier drug wars, officials apparently condoned the flow of narcotics into minority communities to anesthetize black unrest (McCoy, 1984). Now, rather than the drugs themselves, drug warriors may fear the escape from mainstream society that narcotics provide minorities: What will keep them on track? How can officials stop drugs from cultivating rebels (Zappa, 1990)? Either way, the wars seem less against drugs than against African-American youths who, when not killed, find themselves abused and warehoused in prison (Lusane, 1991; Muwakkil, 1989; C. Williams, 1990; Wright, 1990). The government and the media condemn initiatives that actually reduce drug use, such as Louis Farrakhan's Nation of Islam programs: Is it because such programs succeed because of black pride rather than black submission (Morley, 1988)?

Fueling Racism

Drug wars victimize minorities not merely as individuals but also as a group. They promote racism. In an earlier drug war, some federal police officers switched from .22 to .38 caliber pistols because their old ones "couldn't stop coke-crazed black men." (Levine & Reinarman, 1987). Repeated and highly publicized enforcement crackdowns still portray African-Americans as the drug problem even though middle-class whites consume more illegal narcotics (Monteiro, 1990). Consider the dark-skinned showpieces of the White House's wars on crime and drugs: The racism of the Willie Horton furlough ads helped Bush win the election; the staged arrest of Keith Jackson in Lafayette Park launched Bush's drug policy; the drug entrapment of Marion Barry cast doubt on black leadership; and the capture of "drug lord" Manuel Noriega justified the U.S. invasion of Panama (Herman, 1989).

Look who appears in the pictures in *Time* and *Newsweek* reports about the drug problem. We see African-Americans and Latinos: handcuffed, stretched out on the ground, spread-eagle against a wall, in court, or marching off to prison (Hutchinson, 1989). One of William Bennett's top assistants admitted, "It's easier and less expensive to arrest black drug users and dealers than it is whites" (McPherson, 1992). No wonder that we have seen a new wave of hate crimes against African-Americans by white gangs, such as at Howard Beach. And why was a black mayor, Marion Barry, singled out when dozens of other officials are similar abusers? Is this drug control or is it beating back the gains of the civil rights movement?

It is easy for whites to say "I told you so" and oppose affirmative action when African-American communities are portrayed as immoral and black leaders as criminal (Morley, 1990). When Washington, D.C., African-Americans see these double standards and then see white National Guard troops patrolling their predominantly black city, we can imagine why they overwhelmingly support Barry despite his problems. With race relations already poor, do we need drug wars that make them even worse?

Women and Children as Victims

Across economic classes, women and children bear many of the drug wars' worst consequences. They are victimized by policies that help generate their drug use, threaten their lives and health, withhold treatment and alternatives, and police them as if they were hardened criminals. They also bear the victimization that male drug abusers cause: domestic violence, economic insecurity, and deteriorated lives.

The Treatment Gap

The U.S. Department of Justice admits that probably 90% of all drug users want to quit but lack treatment programs. Almost the entire drug-control budget goes to enforcement (Schmoke, 1989). In 1989, 720 drug-exposed babies were born in San Francisco. Their mothers vied for 10 places in live-in drug treatment centers that, when they exist, almost always work. The city's total drug-treatment waiting list stood at 7,000. Only 67 of California's 366 publicly funded treatment centers take women, and only 16 accept the women's children (Johnson & Bielski, 1990). In New York City, 85% of the treatment programs refuse pregnant drug users, thus blocking preventive medicine that could stop addiction from passing to babies (Hoffman, 1990).

Fifteen percent of the 550 applicants turned away monthly by San Francisco's Haight Ashbury Free Clinic attempt suicide. Some women take drugs to withstand the prostitution into which they are forced; others claim they use sex for money to support their untreated drug habits. Some have now contracted AIDS from that sex. By perpetuating drug abuse, withholding treatment alternatives, and opposing needle exchanges, American drug wars have helped to spread AIDS through intravenous drug use, now the disease's leading vehicle (Lazere, 1990a; Schuyler, 1990).

Social Services as Pregnancy Police

At best, pregnant drug users bear the stigma of being viewed as bad mothers. At worst, they are labeled as criminals. Social service agencies increasingly police pregnancies. Many hospitals now must screen newborns for drug symptoms. In Butte County, California, positive tests can be used to prosecute mothers for illegal drug use. Even if they are not imprisoned, mothers who will not discuss their drug behavior with hospitals or prosecutors can be labeled as "uncooperative," and lose their babies to the child welfare system (LaCroix, 1989).

New York City's health department separated 1,325 drug-exposed infants from their mothers after birth in 1986—and 4,268 in 1988 (Maher, 1990). Yet helping pregnant women in residential treatment centers is far cheaper than paying for intensive care for 375,000 new crack babies each year, for child welfare, and for these children's likely disabilities, learning handicaps, and health problems (LaCroix, 1989). Rather than risk criminal prosecution or child separation, some women go into hiding, thus missing prenatal care, perpetuating their drug abuse, increasing home deliveries and damaged babies, and sometimes resorting to self-performed abortions. Most women who lose their children are African-Americans: Doctors turn them over to child-abuse authorities 10 times more often than they do white women (LaCroix, 1989; McPherson, 1992).

Women now risk prosecution not only for their own drug behavior, but also for harms that behavior commits against their children. With a federal Child Abuse During Pregnancy Prevention Act pending, eight states already have laws for charging drug-using, pregnant women with child abuse. Of course, drugs such as alcohol, nicotine, steroids, and pharmaceuticals are excluded.

One woman was convicted of passing drugs to a minor by using them while pregnant; another woman, addicted to crack, was convicted of manslaughter when her twins died after birth (LaCroix, 1989).

Drug Offenders as Victims

While some may abuse themselves and others, drug offenders often are also victims. We barely consider what produced their drug involvement, why it has been labeled criminal, and what consequences they suffer as drug war targets (Balloni, 1988).

Manufacturing Criminals

Double standards determine which drugs and whose drug behavior are defined as criminal. Discrimination continues in who suffers the most serious enforcement and punishments. Drug wars create criminals by definition, criminalizing behavior that could as easily be labeled as illness, susceptibility, or even recreation. This is particularly unjust given U.S. social conditions and cultural patterns. We would be foolish to romanticize drug offenders. Nevertheless, many of them are lured by inadequate education, the appeals of our consumer culture, or the failures of the American dream. Then they are punished for succumbing to the illusory incentives of drug use.

Punishment, Not Treatment

To make matters worse, drug offenders get no help when apprehended. Instead of treatment and education, they receive increasingly more severe punishments. The 1980s crime and drug wars produced a tremendous escalation in prisoners and prison terms. Half the prisoners are there for drug offenses. A new federal law imposes automatic life imprisonment without parole on repeat offenders for minor drug possession (Weinstein & Jones, 1990). Yet punishment achieves no legitimate correctional objectives: no reform, no rehabilitation, no deterrence. Prison reinforces drug abuse: It gives offenders even less to lose, stigmatizes their future opportunities, undermines treatment possibilities, and typically provides more drugs and dealing than takes place outside the prison (Blair, 1990). Prisons serve as abusive, overcrowded warehouses for drug war casualties; inmates serve as prisoners of these wars.

Crime Victims as Victims

Strategically, officials fight crime and drug wars in the name of victims. Yet victims do not benefit; they end up worse off than before.

Increasing Victimization

Drug wars do not work. Because they cannot prevent drug crime from escalating, victimization proliferates. Drug criminalization generates secondary crimes, which are committed to finance drug use and to control drug territories. Enforcement raises not only prices but also the stakes. Escalating profits and increasing risks stimulate desperate measures, producing greater violence, bribery, and even terrorism—victimization that would not otherwise occur (Hamowy, 1987).

Drug wars fail because they target symptoms rather than the sources of crime and drug abuse. They perpetuate, even intensify, the injustices and abuses of power that generate most drug abuse and criminal victimization. Overcriminalization overwhelms the criminal process, paralyzing the police and clogging the courts with drug cases rather than with more serious victimization.

Co-opting Victims

Drug crusades manipulate victims for political objectives. People trade their rights for empty promises of greater police protection. Politicians pit victims against offenders, even though both groups are routinely victimized. Ostensibly promoted to enhance victim rights, such crusades mask the real political agenda of rolling back offender rights, which does nothing to help victims—particulary nothing to reduce their victimization (Siegel, 1989; Walker, 1982). Drug wars co-opt victim movements and frustrate genuine advances. The "official" victims' movement carefully bounds victim initiatives, supporting only those that fit conservative political agendas and law-and-order crime strategies. Government policy marginalizes strategies that are designed to really help victims, particularly when they threaten the status quo and address victimization from a feminist, liberationist, or human rights perspective.

Police as Victims

Law enforcers help impose the victimization that is caused by drug wars. Yet they may themselves be victimized by the role they are expected to play in fighting wars that we will inevitably lose (Elias, 1993c). Some critics compare police officers to U.S. soldiers during the Vietnam War.

Frontline Casualties

As with drug offenders, we need not romanticize police innocence. Nevertheless, law enforcers do not declare drug wars, they merely fight them, unsavory tactics notwithstanding. Police are victimized first by the violence, pressures, and frustrations they suffer on the drug wars' front lines (Hackett, 1989). They become unavoidable targets at home and abroad (Shannon, 1988).

Law-enforcement people are caught in the middle, asked to complete an impossible task. We cannot win a drug war through enforcement, no matter how rigorous (Hayeslip, 1989). If police officers do not know that starting out, they soon learn (Levine, 1990). Why must they risk their lives and safety for worthless crusades? Why risk further alienating people and communities with work that is inappropriate for law enforcement?

Diversions

Drug wars divert police officers, monopolizing half of all police hours, resources, and personnel in most cities (Harris, 1990). This diverts police from addressing more serious crimes and victimization, and it undermines their ability to address such results. As victims, police officers should oppose drug wars. They should reconsider fighting crime wars as well, because they are also futile and ignore crime's social sources. One less counterproductive crusade might lead to another, eventually redefining the police role and the interests it serves.

Drug enforcement provides police officers overwhelming temptations, such as those the drug trade provides people in U.S. ghettos. With enforcement futile and dangerous, law enforcers use more desperate measures, becoming more repressive and violent themselves, constitutional barriers notwithstanding. Indeed, U.S. Supreme Court decisions encourage them. Police officers increasingly break the law to enforce the law.

Law-enforcement agents often get lured into the drug trade themselves, seeing chances to profit far beyond their regular incomes (Moore & Kleiman, 1989). In the mid-1970s, the Knapp Commission declared the New York City Police Department as the city's biggest drug dealer. U.S. police corruption is still extensive: Officers steal, deal, and use drugs and are sometimes allied with criminal drug syndicates (Wozencraft, 1990).

Foreigners as Victims

U.S. drug policies extend far beyond our own borders. We blame our drug problems on foreigners, and then we launch drug wars that bring widespread victimization.

Intervention, Corruption, and Repression

Drug enforcement helps justify U.S. military and other forms of intervention into nations such as Bolivia, Peru, Burma, Pakistan, Laos, Colombia, and Mexico. Even when not in the form of military operations, intervention brings abuse, pillage, and violence, for crusades that do not stem cultivation or production. It can have consequences as serious as the 1,000 dead, 23,000 homeless, and billions in economic damage the U.S. military produced in its invasion of Panama. All of these losses were accrued simply to kidnap a man whose drug involvement was sponsored by the U.S. government—and to replace him with other Panamanians whose banks launder drug money.

With the Cold War over, the military needs new threats to sustain itself: Drug lords have become the new enemy, drug wars the new focus (Rabine, 1989). We have launched military drug operations in Honduras, Bolivia, and Mexico—not to mention our Grenada and Panama invasions—with sanitized code names such as Operation Just Cause. In Colombia, we have pushed for a military landing; in Peru, we are building a military base and have increased military aid 7,000% in one year (Knoll, 1990).

More U.S. military drug campaigns loom ahead for objectives beyond drug control. We are likely to see hit-and-run attacks by U.S. forces against drug laboratories and storage sites, search-and-destroy missions to cripple production, assaults against drug lords' headquarters, and more full-scale counterinsurgency warfare, which is the most important military goal. This low-intensity warfare will not control drugs, and yet, once launched, it might entrench us in a Vietnam-like struggle against an artificial but resilient alliance of drug barons, peasants, and guerilla forces (Collett, 1988; Kawell, 1990; Klare, 1990; Wenner, 1990).

Rather than discouraging foreign drug trade, U.S. drug wars promote it (Wisotsky, 1986). Drug production simply relocates or begins again after our troops leave (Andreas, 1990). Former DEA officers tell us about interagency competition, government lying, phony drug raids, and corruption undermining U.S. enforcement activities (Levine, 1990). Interdiction makes only small dents, and it stimulates contingency markets such as Colombia's new interest in Europe ("It Doesn't Have to Be," 1989).

Combined with foreign development policies that drain rather than add resources, our drug wars have put a premium on drug money in places such as Turkey, Thailand, and much of Latin America. Drug power becomes political power, and foreign governments become corrupted by the drug trade and its control over national politics. The so-called cocaine coup in Bolivia showed drug money capturing politics and providing scarce foreign exchange for reducing that nation's enormous debt (Kwitny, 1987).

U.S. drug wars also promote government repression abroad. To fuel its anticommunist crusade, the CIA has financed itself in the drug trade or ignored drug dealing by pliant Southeast Asian and Central American leaders, even when the drugs are destined for U.S. soldiers and American streets (Corn, 1988; Grietz, 1990; Kruger, 1980; Lusane & Desmond, 1989; McCoy, 1984; Naureckas & Ryan, 1987). For political reasons, the United States ignores Afghanistan's and Pakistan's $5-billion annual drug industry, which supplies one third of our heroin addicts (Blair, 1990). No anticommunist forces have been too repressive for the United States to support. The Iran-Contra scandal showed that one presidential administration itself willingly peddled drugs and scrapped the U.S. Constitution for similar ends.

When U.S. aid seems targeted to genuinely fight drug production, foreign governments often divert it to impose martial law, finance arbitrary arrests, sequester property, and fight "dirty wars" against rebels, peasants, or political opponents (Lernoux, 1988). The Colombian military uses U.S. drug-enforcement aid to terrorize teachers, students, reformers, and human rights advocates, and thus avoids clashes with drug barons (Dermota, 1989; Kirk, 1989; Pearce, 1990). The drug war provides a distraction from the social and economic problems that reformers have targeted (Doyle & Statman, 1988; Garcia Marquez, 1990). Since 1986, 8,000 grassroots activists have been murdered by the Colombian military and its death squads (Arenson & Ginsburg, 1990; Chernick, 1990). Colombia's police forces, which are more directly involved in drug control, have been targeted by a drug lord enforcer who models himself after Sylvester Stallone and trains his paramilitary squads using Rambo movies (Arana, 1990).

Economics and Environment

Drug wars disregard grim economic realties abroad, even though U.S. policy has strongly shaped them. Eradication programs ignore coca culture in places such as Bolivia and Peru, where coca has deep roots and multiple uses in daily life. Some people survive only by using coca, chewing the leaves to numb their lingering hunger. Pope John Paul II lectured Bolivians about drugs and yet downed cup after cup of coca tea during his recent visit.

Coca economics makes cultivation increasingly inevitable. Even with middlemen, coca sales can bring significant profits (Gorriti, 1990). Criminalization artificially sustains coca prices and production, doing nothing to stem the demand (Morales, 1989). The cocaine industry provides 1 of every 3 or 4 jobs in Bolivia. "Crop substitution" programs hardly compete with a good coca crop. Rather than humanitarianism, U.S. aid programs such as Food for Peace exist primarily to dump U.S. surpluses and thus maintain high agribusiness profits. Yet dumping slashes prices for food grown by foreign farmers, undermining their business and pushing even more of them into drug cultivation (McConahay & Kirk, 1989; Ridgeway, 1989).

To fight futile drug wars, we are asking desperate societies to divert scarce resources for enforcement. Asking Peru, for example, to fight a drug war is like asking a nation that is already fighting the Civil War and the Great Depression to take on Prohibition as well (Andreas, 1990). Instead of seriously addressing the economic problems that underlie the drug trade, the Cartegena drug summit served more as a propaganda show ("Drug Summit," 1990).

Foreigners suffer another kind of violence from our drug wars. They are victimized by a deteriorating physical environment that endangers their health and lives. Chemical campaigns unleash poisons such as Spike, 2 4-D, Paraquat, and even Agent Orange onto foreign lands, producing nausea, unquenchable thirst, black and tarry stools, children vomiting blood, increasing elderly death rates, bloated faces, lost sensation in hands and feet, nerve damage, livestock deaths, and cancer (McConahay & Kirk, 1989).

Who's Winning the Drug War?

Why are drug wars repeatedly fought? If they fail to control drugs, and if they create victims and victimization, then who benefits? What are the politics of drug wars that allow some to gain from apparent defeat?

Drug Lords and Dictators

Foreign drug lords win drug wars. Enforcement, although inconvenient, has been largely ineffective against them, compared to smaller players. When interdiction makes small supply cuts, prices and profits actually increase. Drug lords oppose U.S. drug legalization because it would destroy their lucrative, if somewhat dangerous, business. Foreign dictators also win drug wars. Drugs help divert public attention from real social and economic problems, justify extreme measures, fuel repressive campaigns against political opponents, keep foreign aid flowing, and entrench elites in power far longer than they might otherwise have survived.

Dealers, Moralists, and Reactionaries

Like foreign drug lords, futile drug wars benefit many domestic drug dealers, middlemen, and launderers who mostly evade arrest. Like alcohol during Prohibition, the drug trade fuels U.S. organized crime, reaping $50 billion to $60 billion annually (Wenner, 1990). Drug wars help legal drug dealers: The alcohol, tobacco, and pharmaceutical industries avoid competition and legitimize their dangerous drugs. Moralists and opportunists—people such as former drug czar William Bennett, who wants to be president—also win, fueling their holy, political campaigns.

Political retrogrades in both parties, among both liberals and conservatives, also win our drug wars. For defending the status quo at home, drug crusades divert attention from the drug problem's sources and from the U.S. system's deepening failures and injustices. They help those who want to reinforce elite power, unleash police, expand prisons, reverse civil rights gains, roll back offenders' rights, and control women, minorities, and the poor. Drug wars help those who are opposed to structural changes, which threaten their interests but which are essential for seriously reducing victimization in American society (Wisotsky, 1986).

Drug frenzy also helps to preserve the status quo abroad. It legitimizes U.S. interventions. It substitutes for the late Cold War and maintains our military presence. It frees our intelligence agencies for subversion, assassinations, and counterinsurgency against political opponents. It maintains foreign economic dependence and subservience, perpetuating pliant governments and favorable business climates (Wenz, 1989). As a moral crusade, it is designed to repair our damaged reputation in the international arena (Ivans, 1990).

These winners suggest why, having apparently failed, drug wars are nevertheless repeatedly fought. Like the Vietnam War, drug wars are not tragic mistakes committed by well-meaning but misguided officials. We have fought enough of them to know that they do not work. Officials care little about the victims of drug abuse. Instead, drug wars concentrate political power, benefit the few, violate human rights, and block social change.

Peace, Not War

Wars cannot prevent drug abuse; instead they only victimize. Drug wars should have no part in any progressive victim policy or movement. Drugs help us escape reality. When we escape repeatedly, abusing drugs, we must ask, what is wrong with that reality? If we improve that reality, then drug abuse will likely decline (Wisotsky, 1986).

Rather than a war on drug victims, we should be making peace with the drug problem, launching not a war but a peace movement against drug abuse. Such a movement would begin with treatment, education, and rehabilitation —public health measures, not harsh enforcement and punishment (Chambliss, 1989; "Is TV News Hyping," 1990). It would legalize or decriminalize illegal drugs, grant amnesty to drug prisoners, borrow from foreign legalization experiences, and tax and supervise drug sales (Engelsman, 1990; Schmoke, 1989; Yoffe, 1990). It would eliminate drug testing and other rights violations. It would encourage communities to wrest drug and crime policy from ineffective and counterproductive officials. It would start undoing our culture of addiction, beginning with advertising that promotes alcohol, nicotine, and endless consumption (George, 1990; McGrath, 1990; C. Williams, 1990).

Most important, it would approach both drug and crime control as human rights enforcement; it would pursue justice by ending the adverse social conditions that generate crime, drug abuse, and victimization. A peace movement against drug abuse would begin the creation of a more just political, social, and economic system. If the late Soviet Union could admit its problems and pursue fundamental change, then why should the United States not have its own *glasnost* and *perestroika*? Doing so not only will reduce drug victimization, but also will reduce victimization generally.

Instead, U.S. officials will likely perpetuate the policies of the past. They will launch more wars and mobilize even greater force against the scourge of crime and drugs. Punishments also are likely to continue escalating.

Indeed, conventional wisdom conveniently assumes that what victims want most of all is for officials to "throw the book" at offenders. But as the next chapter suggests, this assumption may be all wrong.

6

Do Victims Want Revenge?

[And] this is what works, and what has always worked, among people who care for each other. . . . The offense is viewed as a joint responsibility . . . as a symptom that something is drastically wrong—and that something decisive is needed to correct it. . . . [T]he change called for is the transformation of a criminal justice system based on retaliation and disablement to a system based on reconciliation through mutual restitution.

Richard Korn

The Politics of Punishment

PERIODICALLY, interest is rekindled in alternatives to conventional sentencing and incarceration. This may be motivated by political shifts or by the simple realization that imprisonment does not work: It does not achieve its objectives, and it is counterproductive. Rarely do we alter substantively our sentencing practices; alternatives may be widely discussed, but they are only sporadically implemented. Fears of excessive decarceration are short-lived (Scull, 1983), curtailed by the inevitable return to get-tough strategies from which politicians and bureaucrats get impressive political mileage. The huge build-up in the U.S. prison population during the 1980s, for example, cut short any concerns about correctional "softness" or about the prison system achieving any objective other than brute retribution.

AUTHOR'S NOTE: This chapter is based on Elias, R. (1991). Victim-Based Sentencing: Who Gets What? In L. Samuelson and B. Schissel (Eds.), *Criminal Justice*. Toronto: Garamond.

One apparent difference, however, has emerged in recent years. Instead of considering sentencing alternatives primarily for their effect on offenders, we now consider them in part for their benefits for victims. We hear that sentences should be tailored more to victims' preferences and to the crime's impact on the victim. Restitution previously had been justified for helping rehabilitate offenders; now we justify it more for helping victims. It is used not as a substitute for prison, but as a supplement.

What role should victim-based sentencing play in criminal corrections? Before we can answer, we must first consider the current political and philosophical climate of U.S. criminal justice. While perhaps painful to admit, U.S. crime policy has failed miserably. Periodically, new doses of "law and order" are recycled as new policy with the predictable results—increasing crime and victimization. The reason for this is now also a familiar refrain: Our policies fail because they ignore crime's sources and the fundamental changes needed in U.S. society to eliminate them. We can only understand the possible effectiveness of sentencing alternatives within this context, however formidable or uncomfortable it might be.

The difference in the 1980s was in how victims were more systematically enlisted to promote a new round of conventional crime policy. Helping victims has been the latest justification for redoubling our efforts, our toughness, and our punishments, thereby further eroding our already fragile civil liberties. But has this approach helped victims? It has not reduced crime; it may well have helped increase crime. The approach may have helped create at least the illusion of power for the victims' movement or at least part of the movement. It may have helped victims participate in the criminal process, including sentencing, and yet this may hurt victims more than help them. The approach may have helped victims enhance their rights, but the formality of rights does not guarantee their implementation in practice.

What does this have to do with sentencing alternatives? Under the unlikely scenario that alternatives might be seriously pursued, the best reforms would help victims both indirectly (by reducing crime in the first place) and directly (by tailoring punishments more specifically to victim needs). This is a tall order; what kind of progress have we made?

Conflicting Theories of Victim Participation

What are the possibilities for victim participation in the sentencing process? We can examine several ways in which victims have already been involved.

But what about the theoretical justification for this participation in the first place?

Enhancing the Victim's Role

In recent years, in an environment in which crime policy has been heavily influenced by a new concern for victims, the wisdom of involving victims in the criminal process has been taken for granted. A proliferation of victims' bills of rights in many states assumes that victims have an important role to play. This assumption begins with victims' centuries-old exclusion from a process in which they were once central actors, empowered directly to either find or personally impose some punishment or other solution for specific wrong-doing. When the state emerged and became more prominent in people's lives, the government began to displace the victims' direct role in the criminal process. The sovereign learned that he could take the criminal fines that might otherwise go to the victim. Crimes became viewed as offenses not primarily against victims but as against the state and society.

Advocates of participation claim that victims should have their role restored. Crimes, after all, are felt primarily by those who are directly victimized. Victims, therefore, should have at least a shared role in pursuing, processing, and even punishing offenders (Barlow, 1976). In our rush to aid victims, however, this theoretical justification for victim participation has perhaps not been well examined (Henderson, 1985; Lamborn, 1987b). Or perhaps it hinges on some faulty assumptions about how the criminal process really works.

Questioning the Victim's Role

Skeptics wonder whether there should be some legitimate limitations on victim involvement. For example, many victims' rights have been justified in conflict with defendants' rights. If defendants have rights, then why not victims, too? Yet in practice, defendants may have many fewer rights than we normally assume. Police officers and other criminal-justice personnel often do not honor those rights. Approximately 90% of all criminal cases are plea bargained; here defendants give up their rights in a process that might be unfair and involuntary.

Politically popular claims about "handcuffing the police" and "excessive rights for defendants" fall apart upon inspection (Glasser, 1991; Walker, 1982).

Defendants' rights hardly match the state's power and resources, particularly when guilt rather than innocence is routinely assumed. Adding victims' rights, especially because many of them directly subtract defendants' rights, increases the imbalance and perhaps the injustice (Kelly, 1987; O'Neill, 1984; Viano, 1987). Victims and defendants may not be as different as we assume: Many victims of violence also have been criminal suspects, and vice versa. There may be victims on both sides (Cohen, 1985; Elias, 1990).

Does victim participation also clash with some of our judicial system's fundamental precepts (Anderson & Woodard, 1985; Feeley, 1979; Karmen, 1984)? If we want to assume that defendants are innocent until proven guilty, then should we not limit victims who, understandably enough, presume guilt? This may be especially important because, in practice, police officers, prosecutors, judges, and defense attorneys already assume guilt (Elias, 1990).

Should victims, who might seek maximum punishments, actively participate in a sentencing process that purports to be fair, equitable, and proportionate (McDonald, 1979)? Do victims' rights guarantee them revenge, a conviction, or a particular punishment (Henderson, 1985)? Is the community thereby deprived of its general interests in criminal justice? Have victim participation schemes gone beyond proper limits?

Victim participation may not do victims a service. The victims' rights movement claims that involvement will provide certain benefits. Victims will have the satisfaction of participating in their own cases. They will be helping to bring criminals to justice. They will learn about the process, fulfill their civic duty, and gain more respect for law enforcement. They will feel gratified by being consulted by criminal-justice personnel.

In practice, however, these benefits rarely result. Most victims are alienated by their participation. They can rarely contribute substantively to their case. They learn only that the criminal process is unpredictable, complicated, and illogical. Even with rights, victims are rarely used, or even consulted, in the process (Elias, 1990).

Advocates assume that victims are really needed and wanted in the process—if we could just routinize their participation. Yet prosecutors rarely need victims in their cases, even those few that are not plea bargained. More victim involvement usually interferes with courtroom routines. Officials waste time "cooling out" overanxious victims who rarely have an effective role to play.

The so-called "second victimization" victims suffer comes not from a lack of rights or official consideration, but from the organizational incentives of the court process. Given existing structures, which cannot be overcome by granting victim rights, more victim participation probably will only make things worse. The criminal process serves neither victims nor defendants; it serves officials best of all.

But these theoretical and logistical obstacles to victims' participation need not exclude victims from any meaningful role. Instead, we should devise a substantive involvement beyond the barriers. A sentencing role for victims provides one possibility.

Evaluating Sentencing Participation

Victims can now often participate directly or indirectly in the sentencing process (McLeod, 1986, 1987; Sebba, 1982). This might involve conventional processes such as plea bargaining, formal sentencing, and parole hearings. Or victims might participate in an alternative sentencing process, such as a diversionary program or restitution scheme.

Conventional Sentencing

Plea Bargaining

Victims might participate in plea bargaining, which carries the likelihood of particular sentences in exchange for guilty pleas. Victim advocates want victims to influence whether cases are plea bargained and on what terms. Most criminal cases are plea bargained; victims participate here or they probably will be excluded altogether from the disposition. Twenty-three states have now given victims the right to participate in plea bargaining (NOVA, 1988). Alternatively, some victims' advocates want to eliminate plea bargaining altogether, thus forcing full trials in which victims can participate more directly (Welling, 1987). The President's Task Force on Victims of Crime (1982) called for this approach.

In practice, however, both increasing the victim's role and eliminating plea bargaining altogether are unlikely. Court personnel view victims as outside interferences in the courtroom routine (Davis, 1983). The efficient management of large workloads is the primary motivation for most prosecutors, defense attorneys, and judges (Hall, 1975; McDonald, 1976). And workloads can be managed effectively in our typically overcrowded courts only through plea bargaining. Court officials form work groups in which conflicts and surprises yield to cooperation and predictability (Eisenstein & Jacob, 1977); victims threaten this working relationship and thus are largely excluded (Davis & Dill, 1978; Elias, 1990).

Attempts to impose victims' participation in plea bargaining will be strongly resisted. If such participation is mandated, then court personnel are likely to arrange only perfunctory and meaningless victim involvement. Alternatively, attempts to eliminate plea bargaining altogether will not get far, except perhaps in the few courts with light workloads or uncommonly large resources. Without plea bargaining, most urban courts would grind to a halt; even a small reduction would cripple operations. Court officials are accustomed to plea bargaining; full trials would significantly complicate and expand their work.

Opening, reducing, or eliminating plea bargaining may not benefit victims anyway. Such changes assume that victims will be happier with greater participation; in fact, it may produce greater dissatisfaction instead. Victims are routinely alienated by their participation, even with better services and rights. They are not likely to be called to testify—and if they are, they might find themselves on trial. Even if not grilled by a defense attorney, testifying or otherwise participating might not be very cathartic: It might be counterproductive, producing frustration and delayed healing (Halleck, 1980; Henderson, 1985).

Victim Impact Statements

Should victims have the right to participate in conventional sentencing? Many victims' advocates think so; this right may be the one stressed most. It comes in two forms: victim impact statements and victim statements of opinion (Hoffman, 1983; Varenchik, 1987).

Victim impact statements have been legislated in all but two states. They are written descriptions of the crime's medical, financial, and emotional impact. Probation officers often prepare them to include in their presentence report, which also describes the offender's background and the crime's circumstances. Although the law requires objective statements, some jurisdictions allow victims or advocates to prepare them. Either way, judges use these reports in determining sentences (NOVA, 1988).

Victim statements of opinion allow victims to tell judges what sentence they would like; 35 states have this procedure. This might give victims the right to allocution—that is, orally addressing the sentencing judge. Alternatively, victims might submit a written statement or letter to the judge. Some states allow both impact statements and statements of opinion (NOVA, 1988).

These rights raise many questions. First, can we justify these statements as contributing to legitimate correctional objectives, or do they perhaps even contradict them? Punishment produces little specific or general deterrence. Even if it did, the punishment, not victim involvement, would deter. Imposing incapacitation, another correctional goal, should rely on decisions about the offender not about the victim, because we cannot predict that the offender will strike the same victim if not imprisoned. Victims have no function for rehabilitation, except perhaps in relationship cases; even here victims might legitimately help implement the sentence, but they should not determine it.

Increasingly, we have returned to a traditional, but not necessarily legitimate, correctional goal: retribution (Culhane, 1985; Knopp, 1976). Even if revenge were appropriate in a civilized society, allowing victims to pursue it conflicts with two principles of punishment: equity and proportionality. Retribution also directs itself against offenders instead of against the culture that produces them, which would be a more fruitful target for really eliminating crime (Fattah, 1992c; Henderson, 1985).

Getting more information from the victim to determine punishment may be excessive retaliation. Gradations in the criminal code and the specific charges lodged against offenders already account for relative harm. By law, sentencing has already been tailored to the harm done; integrating the victim's view of harm may undermine it.

Involving victims in retributive sentencing might also backfire. Retribution assesses the offender's blame. Participating victims might find themselves being evaluated for their own blame or for what they might have contributed to the crime. Victims might be accused of provoking the crime, of not taking sufficient precautions, of not resisting enough, and so forth. This might undermine the sentence that the victim seeks (Dussich, 1976; Henderson, 1985).

On the other hand, do victims always want to impose the maximum penalty? Will getting the maximum, and thus achieving revenge, be in the victim's best interests? We have to wonder whether victims pushing for severe penalties do so on their own volition or because they have been incited into the quest for revenge by others (Henderson, 1985), such as those who mobilize victims by insisting that their problems stem from judicial "softness." If revenge is universal, then how do we explain survivors of murdered victims who argue for leniency toward offenders and who oppose the death penalty (Immarigeon, 1991; Pepinsky, 1991b)?

Who benefits when victims demand harshness? Probably not victims: Although forgiveness may be difficult to muster, many observers believe that it will promote a far better resolution and healing for victims than will revenge (Arendt, 1958; Henderson, 1985; Holbrook, 1988). In the current political environment, victim participation for harsher sentences benefits conservative law-and-order advocates far more than victims; even when victims get a chance to participate, they stand to be manipulated for other objectives (Elias, 1984, 1985a). The state generates a sense of revenge, manipulating victims' emotions, but then it robs victims of a meaningful sense of participation in anything but draconian responses. More informal, face-to-face encounters (that is, those that seek responsiveness) with their perpetrators show that victims usually do not want the revenge that officials seem so intent on creating (Pepinsky, 1991a).

Less exploitative, perhaps, would be linking impact statements to alternative sentencing, such as restitution, thus providing more benefits for victims and offenders than for bureaucrats and ideologues (Posner, 1984). Some early evidence on victim participation in sentencing showed that it was not disruptive, that victims were satisfied, and that they were not overly vindictive (Galaway, 1984). Probation officers may also be receptive to the input (McLeod, 1986, 1987). Yet other critics question the experience: Judges may ignore the recommendations in the victim impact statement, thus increasing the victim's frustrations; satisfaction may be better achieved by providing good information and by treating the victim with dignity earlier in the process (Henderson, 1985; Rubel, 1992).

Sentencing often seems to depend on information in the presentence report other than the victim's contribution (Forst & Herndon, 1985). The victim competes with many other parties in determining the final sentence, including legislators, prosecutors, defense attorneys, defendants, probation officers, parole boards, correction officers, state governors, the media, and the general public (Karmen, 1984).

Victim impact statements have been found ineffective in several states. In California, for example, only 3% of the victims use them, and they have a negligible impact on sentencing (Villmoore & Neto, 1987). This ineffectiveness probably stems from the increasing adoption of mandatory and determinate sentencing, another symptom of conservative crime control in the 1980s, which predetermines stiff and rigid penalties. Infrequent victim impact statements may be explained partly by extensive plea bargaining. Should victims be involved in sentencing after the bargain or would that undo the bargain (Feeley, 1979)? If so, it would make plea bargaining much less likely, with devastating consequences for criminal court workloads.

Limits already have been formally placed on victim impact statements. They have been found unconstitutional in capital cases (Sharman, 1988). This ruling might be extended to other instances where the victim's vindictiveness might amount to cruel and unusual punishment. At least one Oregon prosecutor has been sanctioned for discussing the presentence report with victims before submitting their impact statement. This has been labeled "unethical" because it reveals confidential information in the presentence report to victims (Stein, 1988).

Moreover, victims may have no legitimate due process claims at sentencing because they arguably suffer no threatened or actual deprivation at the government's hands (Henderson, 1985). Although obviously unconstitutional, so-called "preventive incapacitation"—the prediction of criminality and the sentencing of likely offenders—gained considerable official support in the early 1980s (Greenwood, 1982). From this, some would have victims claim that sentencing offenders may jeopardize their life, liberty, and property because insufficient punishments might subject them to subsequent attacks by the same offender. Will victim rights at sentencing be an even further erosion of our judicial standards?

Finally, victims have appeared at sentencing indirectly through various victim interest groups. MADD, for example, has launched a campaign in court to monitor judges and their sentencing decisions (Lightner, 1984; Rios & Yeochum, 1983). Judges resent this and regard it as illegitimate interference in their work (Magagnini, 1983). In response, they may get tougher on defendants, but it may not win victims much judicial favor.

Parole Hearings

The offender's ultimate sentence may depend on the outcome of parole hearings. Especially under indeterminate sentencing schemes, offenders may be released early or have their prison terms extended. Here is another opportunity for victims to influence the punishment process.

Assuming that offenders get out too early, that parole boards are overly lenient, and that victims should be allowed to lengthen prison terms, 38 states have allowed either victim impact statements or in-person victim participation at parole hearings, although sometimes only for victims of violence (NOVA, 1988).

A few states require victim notification of hearings by either letter or newspaper notice (Stark & Goldstein, 1985); over time, locating victims can be very difficult (Austern, 1987). State laws vary on public access to parole hearings. Florida and Nevada require access, while at least six other states merely allow it (NOVA, 1988). At hearings, victims might oppose release, claiming that punishment should last longer, based on the harm done by the crime. Or victims might accept release in exchange for restitution or other conditions imposed on the offender (Karmen, 1984).

Are the assumptions underlying victim participation in parole decisions justified? Why should victims have the right to participate (Jobson, 1983)? Here we encounter the same concerns we saw earlier about victim participation in the original sentencing: As with sentencing legislation, gradations of harm are already built into parole rules. Why should victims supersede those rules with their own view of the appropriate punishment?

Do parole boards really favor offenders as victims' advocates believe? Some offenders are released early—but almost always after serving far more severe punishments than those imposed in most other nations. Just as often, offenders are denied release with little justification and no due process (Culhane, 1985). The presidential task force called for open hearings to keep parole boards accountable to victims and the public, and yet the boards' secrecy was more likely to deprive offenders. The increase in suits against parole boards in recent years may make parole release even less likely (Galaway, 1984).

Having been targeted as too lenient with offenders, the use of parole has declined so much that it has been eliminated in the federal system and severely curtailed on the state level: Only 43% of all prisoners are released on parole, down from 72% in the 1970s (Karmen, 1984). This happens even though paroled offenders have a lower recidivism rate than do nonparoled offenders (Michalowski, 1985). Does this shift help past and future victims? If heeded at parole hearings, do victims really benefit, psychologically or physically, from longer punishments? If not, then who benefits from the increased toughness associated with either structurally curtailing parole or with encouraging victims to oppose it in individual cases? Victims may have a legitimate interest in knowing when their offender is released, but generally parole participation may be another instance of the political manipulation of victims for other ends.

Sentencing Alternatives

Diversion

Some jurisdictions have become increasingly interested in diversionary programs as an alternative way of processing criminal cases. This has emerged partly through the "alternative dispute resolution" movement (Karmen, 1984), which has brought the promotion of mediation and community justice centers by conflict-management professionals. Diversionary programs also have gained favor with some criminal-justice actors, because they might help reduce workloads and eliminate cases that either do not belong in the criminal process or will routinely not runs its course. Many relationship cases end, for example, with the apparent victim eventually dropping the charges.

Diversionary schemes have been promoted by the American Arbitration Association, the American Bar Association, the Institute for Mediation and Conflict Resolution, the National Institute for Dispute Resolution, the U.S. Association for Victim Offender Mediation, and the Vera Institute of Justice, as well as by local bar associations or governments. By the late 1980s, nearly 300 programs were operating (American Bar Association [ABA], 1987). The kinds of conflicts accepted by these programs have steadily expanded and now include ongoing feuds, incidents of shared responsibility, minor misdemeanors, and even violent relationship cases. The process, which avoids the formalities of criminal law and courts, ranges from conciliation (promoting an exchange of information) to mediation (promoting face-to-face discussion and compromise), arbitration (promoting a third-party resolution), and counseling (promoting psychological adjustment) (Abel, 1982; Alper & Nichols, 1981; Harrington, 1985; Karmen, 1984).

Aside from serving professional objectives, what do victims get from diversionary programs? The disadvantages may begin with those victims who believe they are completely blameless and prefer individual justice over community objectives. Some victims want guilt to be established. They also want to avoid opening up their own behavior to scrutiny, although this may also happen in regular trials. Some victims may not want to confront their victimizers. Others may not want to compromise, as diversion usually requires. They might want retaliation or revenge; because it shuns punishment, diversion prevents this (Garofalo & Connelly, 1980; Karmen, 1984).

Yet diversion's advantages for victims seem to be many. Conflicts often are more breakdowns in relations than real crimes: Repairing damages may be more appropriate than retaliation. Diversion allows disputants to break down stereotypes, show their feelings, and heal emotional wounds: It ensures that their view will be heard. It prevents the dispute from becoming a zero-sum game with an inevitable winner and loser. It empowers participants instead of having them rely on officials, rules of evidence, and legal jargon. Diversion is cheaper, speedier, and more accessible. Instead of dwelling on the past, it focuses on the future and how hostilities might be eradicated and harmony promoted (Karmen, 1984; Umbreit, 1985a; Wright, 1985, 1991).

In practice, various diversionary schemes have worked well. They have been extended to the full range of criminal offenses. Victims often believe that the programs adequately resolve their disputes. They rate mediators as being more fair than judges. The settlements are fulfilled more often than are court judgments. Confrontations are minimal, and victims often find their contact with offenders productive. Most victims claim they would participate again in such processes (Cook, Roehl, & Sheppard, 1980; Davis, Tichane, & Grayson, 1980; Garofalo & Connelly, 1980; Tomasic & Feeley, 1982; Umbreit, 1986; Wahrhaftig, 1979).

Restitution

Whereas diversionary programs avoid the criminal process, other sentencing alternatives provide substitutes for conventional fines and imprisonment after criminal trials. Some judges have been particularly innovative, devising sentences such as forcing landlords to live in slum housing. But these innovations are uncommon, and most judges do not consider alternatives in the first place.

Restitution provides an important exception. Offenders repay victims with money or services; or they might be ordered to recompense symbolic victims with money or services to the community or payments to a state compensation fund (Galaway, 1977; Klein, 1988). Restitution can be arranged at any stage of the criminal process. It may be part of a diversionary program that avoids trial. It might be used to settle a case before the trial ends or as a part of a plea bargain. Most often, judges order restitution after conviction as a part of probation, suspended sentences, imprisonment, work release, and parole (Newton, 1976).

Judges have long had the power to order restitution, but they rarely do so without specific restitution schemes such as victim-offender reconciliation projects or others found in victim and witness programs or probation departments. Recently, more states have given restitution attention: In 26 states, judges must order restitution unless they provide written explanations why they will not. Restitution has been called for by the federal Victim and Witness Protection Act (NOVA, 1988). There may be as many as 800 juvenile and 500 adult restitution programs across the United States (Harland, 1983; Karmen, 1984). At least 32 reconciliation programs resolve as many as 2,400 cases per year (Umbreit, 1985b).

Some critics question the value of restitution in either principle or practice. It may switch penal policy too much away from society and toward the victim. It may undermine consistent, predictable sentencing if judges use restitution creatively. If not checked, it may let off wealthier offenders more easily and discriminate against poorer offenders. Restitution may be appropriate in only a small number of cases. Offenders may lack the resources or be unwilling to pay. Prison pay is low, and criminal records might limit outside employment. Monitoring and enforcement have not been systematic (Harland, 1982; Karmen, 1984).

Other observers wonder whether restitution conflicts with other correctional objectives such as deterrence, treatment, incapacitation, rehabilitation, and punishment. Because restitution orders have few procedural protections, offenders might be ordered to pay back inappropriate amounts. Restitution may not achieve the other benefits (beyond repayment) that are sometimes attributed to it. Finally, restitution might conflict with the resurgence of get-tough crime policy, which calls for determinate sentencing, more imprisonment, and longer terms (Scutt, 1982).

Defenders of restitution, however, argue that it can achieve many objectives simultaneously. It may help victims by repaying them and restoring them psychologically. It may help offenders by confronting them with the damage they have done and by giving them opportunities to help repair it. It may help society by making prisons less crowded, unburdening government compensation programs, and inducing greater victim participation in criminal justice, while also contributing to penal objectives such as reform, punishment, and rehabilitation (Abel & Marsh, 1984; Knopp, 1976; McGillis, 1986).

Reconciliation programs have worked well in both Canada and the United States (Dittenhoffer & Ericson, 1992; Knopp, 1976; Schneider, 1990; Umbreit, 1986; Welsh, 1990; Wright, 1991; Wright & Galaway, 1989). Victims often seem receptive to alternative sentencing (Henderson & Gitchoff, 1980), and restitution could be increasingly incorporated into victim impact statements (Posner, 1984). Restitution might also work well for serious crimes (Hubbell, 1987).

Although restitution might have drawbacks, it has the advantage of helping us avoid worse and even counterproductive correctional strategies. Now restitution is ordered mostly to supplement imprisonment. It would work much better as a complete substitute for prison. Incarceration significantly lessens the victim's chances of being restituted, and it produces far worse consequences for offenders themselves, who are more likely to respond by committing more crimes after release.

Restitution's reconciliation goal might either fail or be omitted in practice. Offenders might understand the harm they do and yet be unable to erase the years of violence and degradation to which they have often been exposed. Reconciliation might perpetuate stereotypes about deviant individuals instead of examining social injustices and criminogenic environments. Even with these imperfections, however, restitution would still serve victims, offenders, and the society far better than filling up more prisons (Forer, 1980; Knopp, 1976).

Victim-Based Alternatives

Victim Politics

The victims' movement had its greatest impact in the 1980s, achieving significant increases in victims' rights and programs. Yet the victims' movement really consists of several movements, not all of which have shared the same fortunes. "Unofficial" victims' movements, largely blocked by conservative American politics, include the feminist, anticorporate, antiracist, and human rights movements for victims of crime and other injustices. The "official" victim movement, which enjoyed so much success, was fueled largely by conservative law-and-order politics that often ignored or even produced other kinds of victimization (Henderson, 1985).

Although gaining a few benefits themselves, victims have largely been manipulated to promote a new round of get-tough crime policies: Purportedly to protect victims better, a rollback of rights and massive new incarceration have been justified (Smith & Freinkel, 1988; "Victim Rights Bill," 1982). In practice, offenders now have it worse, and yet we have done nothing to reduce the sources of their criminality.

Protections against preventive detention, illegal searches, and coerced confessions—which we would all want if we were accused of crime—have been seriously eroded in a zero-sum game that falsely assumes that victims' rights can come only at the expense of offenders' rights (O'Neill, 1984; Rudovsky, 1988; Viano, 1987). Despite the reforms, victims still suffer, and victimization has increased (Ellison, 1982). Only elites and bureaucrats seem to have bene-fited (Karmen, 1984; "The Illusion of Victim Rights," 1989; "Victim Rights Laws," 1987).

How can we promote victim interests without risking their manipulation or co-optation (Viano, 1987)? What kind of victim participation in criminal justice can really be justified? What kind of victim role in sentencing, in particular, will bring the biggest benefits for all concerned? Perhaps we can simultaneously promote genuine victims' interests, penal reforms, and crime reduction.

Victim Participation

Victims should be able to participate more in the criminal process, but doing so should serve victims rather than officials. Despite their increasing rights, victims will nevertheless be kept from meaningful participation by various organizational constraints. Participation probably will only increase their frustration and victimization and delay their psychological healing. Legitimate concerns about protecting defendants' rights and achieving social (and not merely individual) objectives will further limit victims in the criminal process. To prevent further damage, while also promoting their justifiable interests, victims must participate selectively—that is, enough to gather in-formation and to influence, but not determine, case outcomes.

Sentencing, either early or late in the process, may be a good place for victim participation, but such involvement must be a role that is substantially different from the one the official victim movement now advocates. Partici-pation should help victims and also achieve other important objectives.

Victims and Alternative Sentencing

As suggested, victim participation in conventional sentencing, from plea bargaining to post-trial sentencing and parole hearings, seems largely coun-terproductive. Victims either feel frustrated by organizational barriers or sur-mount them and thereby threaten constitutional protections and even their own recovery. They are unlikely to benefit from rigid bureaucracies, legal crusades, and personal revenge. Conventional sentencing promotes one primary objective: imprisonment. Because this end result provides victims with no demonstrable benefit, they might be best off not participating at all.

In contrast, victim participation in alternative sentencing holds more promise. Diversion and restitution programs provide victims with several possible benefits. They prevent further victimization in the formal criminal process and allow victims more control over cases—not at offenders' expense, but in place of officials. They allow a reconciliation and a settlement that benefit victims more than watching offenders go off to prison. They increase the chances that victims will be repaid in some way for their losses. Because alternative sentencing reduces recidivism, victims have less chance of being victimized again. Diversion and restitution can also be used to redirect conventional processes such as plea bargaining, routine sentencing, and parole hearings toward greater victim objectives.

Decarceration

But victim-based, alternative sentencing helps not merely victims, but also offenders and future victims. Conventional sentencing and imprisonment have failed as public policy. Periodic new bursts of toughness have made the penal process even more counterproductive. By now, the drawbacks are well known. Prisons do not achieve their objectives. They do not deter, reform, or rehabilitate, and thus they do not reduce crime; indeed, imprisonment correlates with an increase in crime both inside and outside prison walls (Darnell, Else, & Wright, 1979; Groves & Newman, 1986; Shapiro & Gutierrez, 1982).

Prisons do punish—not only by the term imposed, but also by the deprivations, injustices, poor conditions, and maltreatment that prisoners suffer (Irwin, 1981; Ryan, 1985). Even if a legitimate objective in a civilized society, punishment undermines our other penal goals. Even many prison wardens admit that only a select few inmates provide any threat to the public. Either we have been willingly supporting failure for no good reason or prisons serve other, more political functions such as warehousing surplus populations (Reiman, 1984; Vogel, 1983). Either way, the victim movement should not be manipulated into supporting the conventional penal system. Prison abolitionists are often portrayed as favoring offenders over victims, yet this belies their frequent support for victims and their persuasive analysis that suggests that reducing (not increasing) criminal punishments may help victims most of all (Pepinsky, 1991a).

Victims will not be the only ones who benefit from sentencing alternatives. Reducing imprisonment also will help offenders and help reduce crime further. We need both *excarceration* (prison substitutes) and *decarceration* (prison depopulation) (Culhane, 1985; Sommer, 1976). The organizational obstacles to change may be as formidable as the political obstacles, but they must be faced, as they have in other nations that already have vastly reduced their prison populations (Harland & Harris, 1984; Knopp, 1976).

Reform, Human Rights, and Political Change

Victim-based sentencing alternatives might promote other changes as well. If routinely practiced, such alternatives might help us alter the criminal process. Currently it helps neither victims nor offenders. In practice, the process usually takes the inquisitorial approach and assumes guilt. Thereafter, it is only a matter of what level of guilt will be set in the plea bargains that typically resolve most U.S. cases. Routine overcharging and the assumption of guilt before plea bargaining provide defendants with few benefits. Organizational incentives make victims into potential obstacles to smooth bargaining; officials try to exclude them. Thus the inquisitorial approach also provides victims with few benefits.

In the remaining cases, where courts use an accusatorial approach at full trial, the state's full weight falls on the defendant, which is why most cases that reach trial end in convictions. But the accusatorial approach also increases the victim's chances of being put on trial, if he or she is used at all. Even with a defendant's conviction and punishment, a victim often emerges even more embittered and degraded.

Some critics believe we can do better than picking between either the inquisitorial or accusatorial approaches. A third way may be imbedded in victim-based sentencing alternatives. Diversion, restitution, and reconciliation programs substitute participatory, empowering, flexible, unwritten, and commonsense procedures for the formality, coldness, rigidity, elitism, and bureaucracy of the conventional criminal process. Despite our traditions, conflict—at least officially supervised conflict (see Christie, 1977)—and zero-sum games may not produce the best justice (Spence, 1988; Strick, 1979; Viano, 1987). As Andrew Karmen (1984) has suggested:

> The growing interest in informal justice is fostered by several beliefs: that centralized governmental coercion has failed as an instrument of social change; that people

must solve their own problems in decentralized, community-controlled forums; that nonstranger conflicts ought to be diverted from the formal adjudication process whenever possible; that both punishment and rehabilitation have failed to "cure" offenders; and that criminal-justice officials and agencies primarily serve the state's interests, or their own, to the detriment of both victims and offenders. (p. 347)

Of course, these strategies and changes would work best if accompanied by a far more serious campaign against victimization's real sources (Elias, 1993b). Internal reforms may prevent the problem from getting worse, but they will not address the fundamental social conditions that underlie most crime. Crime-control strategies that blame offenders, administrative weaknesses, or even victims divert our attention from the far more important systemic sources of crime (Elias, 1993b).

Rather than directing victims against offenders, we would be better off recognizing how victims and offenders are both victims of policies and conditions that largely benefit the few and promote injustice for the many. In passing its Declaration on the Victims of Crime and Abuses of Power, the United Nations has recognized the connection between official or elite policies and a wide range of victimization. As such, it recognizes that genuine crime victims' movements are really human rights movements and are based on a concern for the rights of everyone and on how unjust political and economic conditions produce the victimization we commonly call "crime" (Elias, 1985a).

No sentencing strategy concerned with more than merely internal tinkering can ignore these conditions. To do so dooms penal policy to perpetual failure. Thus, while we consider sentencing alternatives, we also must seriously consider political alternatives. Can we thereby fundamentally reconstitute U.S. crime control? As suggested in the next chapter, the answer might lie in turning conventional policy on its head.

7

Controlling Victimization

WAR OR PEACE?

Loose talk about war against crime too easily infuses the administration of justice with the psychology and morals of war. . . . The process of waging war, no matter how it is rationalized, is a process of moral deterioration.

Felix Frankfurter

[T]he crimes committed in the name of the state, unfortunately, have . . . been so great that we cannot shun the obligation to examine the grounds of its authority and subject them to rigorous critique.

Robert Paul Wolff

W E are a nation at war with ourselves: a civil war. The war of law enforcement against the forces of crime. We imagine this, however cynically, as a conflict between good and evil in which only superior firepower will ensure our security and win the day. We imagine the same things when we attack Panama, Grenada, or Iraq. In an article titled "Moving into the New Millennium: Toward a Feminist Vision of Justice," Kay Harris describes this "civil war" this way:

[It] is the domestic equivalent of the international war system. One has only to attend any budget hearing at which increased appropriations are being sought for war efforts—whether labeled as in defense against criminals, communists or other enemies—to realize that the rationales and the rhetoric are the same. The ideologies of deterrence and retaliation; the hierarchical, militaristic structures and institutions; the incessant demand for more and greater weaponry, technology, and fighting forces; the sense of urgency and willingness to sacrifice other important interests to the cause; the tendency to dehumanize and objectify those defined as foes; and the belief in coercive force as the most effective means of obtaining security. . . . People concerned with international peace need to recognize that supporting the "war on crime" is supporting the very establishment, ideology, structures, and morality against which they have been struggling. (Harris, 1991, pp. 90-91)

What are the ideologies and structures that link how we pursue both national and domestic security? How does each system help generate the violence it then seeks to violently destroy? Why does war fail; how can peace succeed instead? How can we begin to see real crime control not as war, but as a peace movement?

Crime, Violence, and War

Do we need reminders of American society's overwhelming violence? Murders, muggings, beatings, battering, and sexual assaults represent the violence we define as crime. Workplace injuries and disease; environmental pollution and illness; unsafe food, pharmaceuticals, and other products; unnecessary surgery and irresponsible emergency care represent more violence that we usually do not define as crime despite its even greater victimization. Contact sports, children's play, and most of our entertainment media represent the violence of U.S. culture. Domestic repression, prison torture, capital punishment, drug experiments, forced sterilization, and police raids and brutality represent the state's own violence. And hunger, malnutrition, homelessness, untreated illness, and other symptoms of poverty represent the structural violence of American society. Arguably, these are all crimes that are committed in a society that is more than capable of preventing most of this victimization.

Officials target crime and violence very selectively, however, focusing primarily on wrongdoing, which can be blamed on evil individuals or even on careless victims—anything to divert our attention from official wrongdoing and the systemic causes or manifestations of violence. When the government periodically renews its efforts to fight crime—street crime, not domestic or suite crime—war is predictably its strategy, violence its means. We declare wars repeatedly on crime and drugs, even though these wars are never won; we can easily predict that they will be lost.

Mainstream crime policy uses war purportedly to create peace. It has even appropriated the word "peace" to justify its wars. At U.S. military bases, the motto is, "Peace is our profession." "Peacekeepers" are the means. Likewise, police officers are now often called "peace" officers. Nevertheless, military and law-enforcement policies remain the same: They still pursue war, not peace. As a process, crime wars undermine both *negative peace*—the absence of war and violence—and *positive peace*—the provision of political, economic, and social justice (that is, human rights) (Galtung, 1980). Such wars use violence and rights violations as their major tactics. The need to win rationalizes the use of illegitimate, but supposedly more effective, methods. We are told that police should no longer be "handcuffed," that rights must be sacrificed; our enforcement and punishments must be more violent. In the long run, the theory holds, crime will decline and peace will reign (President's Task Force on Victims of Crime, 1982). Yet the peace never comes: *Criminal* violence keeps pace with escalating *official* violence (Caulfield, 1991).

Despite these wars, criminal victimization continues because conventional crime policy either ignores or misdiagnoses the sources of crime and violence (Turpin & Elias, 1992). Officials blame criminals as evil individuals; or they blame institutions for lax enforcement, inadequate resources, and excessive rights and softness; or they even blame victims for not taking proper precautions. Predictably, crime-control strategies follow from these diagnoses. They are pursued; they fail (Anderson, 1988; Pepinsky & Jeslow, 1984; Walker, 1985).

Nevertheless, officials return to these strategies time and again. The diagnoses of the causes of crime necessarily constrict the options for controlling it; Make the wrong diagnoses and you probably will pursue the wrong strategies. Conventional crime policy's repeated failure would seem reason enough to consider alternatives.

Disturbing the Peace

Blaming Culture

An alternative crime policy would wage peace, not war. It would begin with a different diagnosis. Crime primarily results not from inherently evil offenders, institutional inefficiencies, or victim complacency. Rather, it is caused by adverse or destructive political, economic, and social conditions that induce crime across the spectrum of classes and races in U.S. society. Instead of blaming offenders, institutions, or victims, this diagnosis blames the system: the existing set of U.S. political and economic arrangements (Gitlin, 1992). Inadequacies in the U.S. political economy, which are now deeply embedded in U.S. culture, provide the breeding grounds for most crime (Elias, 1990; Gordon, 1990; Stenson & Cowell, 1991). The result is an "unresponsive" society in which those who hold power will not take responsibility for how their policies cause most of society's crime and violence (Pepinsky, 1991a).

The economic system, for example, promotes crime by producing poverty, inequality, homelessness, hunger, and other forms of victimization (Barlett & Steele, 1992). It is not surprising that many poor people turn to crime either for economic gain (as one of their few opportunities) or merely to vent their frustrations (Barlow, 1988; Braithwaite, 1979; Lynch & Groves, 1989; Michalowski, 1985; Silberman, 1978; Wideman, 1984). The economy also promotes excessive materialism, competition, alienation, and consumerism. It pushes us to consider one another as throwaway commodities. To get ahead and keep ahead, middle- and upper-class people also commit crime and violence. If their wrongdoing were measured in the same way as poor people's crimes, then we would find that it amounts to far more violence and damage than the conventional crimes we worry so much about (Frank, 1985; Green & Berry, 1985; Hills, 1987; Hochstedler, 1984; Jones, 1988; Mokiber, 1988; Reiman, 1984).

The political system also promotes crime through its own set of failures, which are induced partly by the economic system (Barak, 1991; Zinn, 1990). Government officials routinely commit crimes themselves, usually with little or no accounting; the Iran-Contra scandal and the savings-and-loan crisis are only two recent examples (Chambliss, 1989; Foraker-Thompson, 1988; Greider, 1992; Kelman & Hamilton, 1989; Kwitny, 1987; Ratner, 1987; Tushnet, 1988; Vankin, 1991). Access to meaningful political participation is blocked for almost all but the very wealthy. Elections function more to tame the masses than to empower them. Despite talk about getting government off our backs, it steadily centralizes and grows. We are overwhelmed and alienated by our various public and private bureaucracies, including most of our workplaces (Slater, 1991). Government pays lip service to equality while tolerating or promoting racism, classism, and sexism—such as the recent Senate victimization of Anita Hill during the Supreme Court confirmation hearings for

Clarence Thomas (Dunbar, 1984; Gross, 1980; Marable, 1983; Parenti, 1988; Russell & Van den Ven, 1984). Institutionalized patriarchy victimizes women in both their personal and public lives. Whether in its domestic or its foreign policy, we learn by official actions that wrongdoing and violence are actually legitimate (Herman, 1982; Rubin, 1986; Wolfe, 1978).

In practice, we lack both political and economic democracy. Our system produces problems and conditions that breed crime far more than do the things we usually blame.

Crime and Repression

But the problems of failed political and economic democracy are the sources of more than merely criminal victimization: The problems are themselves victimization. Human rights advocates would call these problems—this political and economic victimization—*repression*; international law requires nations to prevent or deal with these problems. Nations that fail to do so (particularly if, like the United States, they have the means) are human rights violators (Fattah, 1989). Many of these conditions are crimes against humanity. Thus, we can understand repression as crime and crime as repression—repression that results from the human rights violations produced by unjust political and economic arrangements (Meier & Geis, 1978; Reasons, 1982). As Charles Silberman (1978) argues, "Crime threatens the social order in the same way as totalitarianism" (p. 278).

Criminals are also victims. Of course, offenders bear responsibility for their crimes; viewing criminals as passive automatons shaped by monolithic forces degrades offenders every bit as much as our conventional criminal process. Recognizing offenders' motivations does not excuse their crimes. Nevertheless, offenders act within an environment that often makes crime a viable alternative, a likely possibility—even a necessity. It is not an environment of lenience, as so-called law-and-order advocates argue: For most crimes, the United States has long had the world's highest conviction and incarceration rates and the most severe punishments (Elvin, 1991; Mauer, 1991). Rather, it is an environment of victimization that beats people down, makes them insensitive to one another, numbs them to violence, robs them of opportunities, and provokes their rage, frustration, and desperation. In response, they attack others. Except for hate crimes and sexual and domestic assaults, their victims are often much like themselves: Most victims of violent crimes come from

the same backgrounds as their assailants, and many have themselves committed crimes for similar reasons (Elias, 1990).

It is politically convenient for officials to pit criminals and victims against
each other: Protecting victims has justified our growing fortress mentality,
increased government repression, and led to declining individual rights
(Gordon, 1990; McShane & Williams, 1992; Phipps, 1986). Yet victim policy
does not reduce crime; it may make victimization even more likely. Successful crime control relies not on promoting victims over offenders, but on recognizing how both are victimized and how the rights of both must be protected.
Victims and criminals have the same interests: the protection of their human
rights.

Alternative crime-control strategies would follow from this diagnosis. It
would require us to reduce or eliminate crime's systemic sources. In doing
so, we would be promoting both positive and negative peace. We would see
a reduction in the violence directly produced by the system and its major
institutions and a reduction in the violence committed by others in society
in response to systemic and injustice. By pursuing justice, we would be pursuing
peace; we also would be reducing the crime that now significantly impedes
that peace.

Resisting Peace

Why does mainstream crime policy, which routinely fails, shun this alternative? It does so because it would clash dramatically with the U.S. system's
conventional political and economic practice both at home and abroad. To
adopt alternative crime policies, we would have to stop manipulating or
blaming victims and take victimization (criminal and otherwise) seriously.
We would have to reject democracy for the few in favor of a more just
political economy. We would have to renounce our rejection of international
law and human rights standards (Chomsky, 1988; Falk, 1981; Parenti, 1988;
Reiman, 1984).

Old World Order

The United States has long crusaded as democracy's champion at home and
abroad. It has held up its own system as the democratic ideal and justified
its foreign policy as helping others become more democratic. In practice,

however, the United States does neither. Whether it is our promotion of increasing poverty, homelessness, inequality, and violence at home or our promotion of brutal repression abroad, the victimization produced by U.S. policy hardly makes our commitment to human rights credible (Chomsky & Herman, 1979; "Domestic Surveillance," 1989; Goldstein, 1978; Gross, 1980; Klare & Arnson, 1981; Scherer & Shepard, 1983; Weisband, 1989).

The United States is out of step with the world community (Boyle, 1988; Frappier, 1984; Weston, 1987). We pull out of United Nations' agencies while other nations commit themselves more fully. We are practically alone in rejecting the Law of the Sea Treaty's cooperative exploration of the oceans, alone in defending the unconscionable marketing of infant baby formula, and alone in supporting such pariah states as El Salvador, Chile, Israel, and South Africa. We stand alone in opposing and undermining meaningful environmental initiatives such as those presented at the recent Rio Conference. We increasingly reject and violate international law (and the jurisdiction of agencies such as the World Court), while most other nations increasingly embrace it. We substitute military intervention for diplomacy and nonviolent sanctions, cynically manipulating the United Nations, such as in the recent Gulf War, and perpetuating our culture of violent "solutions" (Clark, 1992; Elias, 1993a).

Human Rights Rhetoric

The United States exhibits a limited commitment to international human rights standards (Claude & Weston, 1989; Forsythe, 1989). By now, the world's nations have recognized, and most have ratified, three "generations" of human rights: political and civil rights; economic, social, and cultural rights; and peace, development, and environmental rights. Until very recently, the United States had ratified none of them. Reluctantly, we have finally endorsed the Covenant on Political and Civil Rights, which comes closest to our own narrow human rights definitions. Although it embodies much of our own Bill of Rights, it adds other rights and threatens to make the rights substantively enforceable and not merely rhetorical. We will have to see whether ratification causes us to take these rights any more seriously. Instead of piecemeal, impermanent, and often unenforced rights protections (Scheingold, 1974), we are responsible for more honestly and equitably guaranteeing freedom of expression, political access, privacy, due process for suspects and defendants, and race and gender equality. Instead, these kinds of rights have declined and are further threatened by the current Rehnquist-led U.S.

Supreme Court. For example, rather than stopping (as the human rights covenants require) California's reinstitution of the death penalty—through its brutal execution of Robert Alton Harris—the Court instead endorsed the killing and blocked additional appeals (Curry, 1988; Dorsen, 1984; Karp, 1988; Lobel, 1988; Marx, 1988; Pell, 1984; Spence, 1988).

Even more ominous for the American system would be to protect the second and third generations of human rights. Embracing economic, social, and cultural rights, for example, would force the United States to fundamentally change its political economy, which now acts systematically to deprive these rights for most people. We can imagine why officials will not recognize the right to housing, employment, quality education, nutrition, good working conditions, comprehensive health care, and social and cultural equality. Similarly, the newest generation of human rights—the rights to peace, development, and a clean environment—also clash with the U.S. system because the rights would condemn our persistent and far-flung military and economic interventionism, reject our vast nuclear stockpiles, and indict the government-condoned corporate pollution of our environment.

Human rights covenants are treaties in U.S. and international law. If ratified, they would become the law of the land under the U.S. Constitution. The rights they contain would be legally enforceable in U.S. courts. We can imagine the threat posed to the U.S. system by suits brought to demand that these rights be protected. Suppose claims were brought by 4 million homeless Americans pursuing their rights for housing, or by our 60 million illiterates seeking their educational rights, or by millions of jobless people (50% in our ghettos) for their rights to employment, or by our 30 million underfed citizens for their nutrition rights, or by millions of underinsured or uninsured (50% of the population) for their health care rights, or by even millions more (such as those living near our 75,000 toxic dump sites) for their environmental rights. Or suppose U.S. citizens or foreigners sued to protect the rights of the millions of people who have been victimized by the repression and economic deprivation exported by our foreign policy to the many nations such as Guatemala, Zaire, and South Korea?

Rights as Threats

Despite the rhetoric, the United States has been only minimally committed to the protection of human rights. The few exceptions are politically motivated, such as the "demonstration elections" we have sponsored to help sanitize our client states (Brodhead & Herman, 1987). When we back away from the endless dictators that we have either sponsored or installed, it has only been after they have outlived their usefulness (such as Manuel Noriega in Panama) or where their popular overthrow is inevitable (such as Ferdinand Marcos in the Philippines). If popular revolution (such as in Sandinista Nicaragua) threatens to seriously protect human rights and promote political and economic democracy, then we attack it.

A nation that tolerates and even promotes the victimization caused by repression can hardly be expected to respond differently to the victimization caused by crime. A nation willing to systematically "batter" Central Americans can hardly be expected to take seriously the "battering" of U.S. women (Tifft & Markham, 1991). Wars on crime and drugs, government-sponsored victim movements, and pious rhetoric about the "forgotten" victim in the criminal process achieve little for crime victims in practice. Little evidence suggests that officials ever thought they would (Elias, 1990; Fattah, 1989).

We do not take crime and its victims seriously for the same reasons that we do not take repression and its victims seriously: To do so would require fundamental changes in the U.S. system, upsetting its prevailing concentration of power and resources. Undoing that concentration is the only hope for genuinely protecting and providing human rights; short of that, crime and other victimization will continue unabated. The United States cannot achieve peace if it is only willing to fight wars, especially because they are often launched not just against innocent foreigners, but also against our own people. Our wars on drugs—which are likely to escalate as we search for Cold War substitutes—directly link our foreign violence and domestic violence, our foreign intervention into Third World nations abroad, and our domestic intervention into Third World communities at home (Elias, 1993a). Are U.S. wars, whether against domestic crime or foreign enemies, fought to promote democracy for the many or to preserve social control and democracy for the few?

A Peace Movement Against Crime

If justice and human rights are the proper crime-control agenda, then peace, not war, must be the means. We need a peace and human rights movement against crime that turns conventional crime policy on its head. It must promote more than reforms; it must bring fundamental social change. Only then will victims—of both crime and repression—see significant improvements in their quality of life.

We need a new vision, not for a utopian society purged of all crime, but for a new culture in which we have taken serious steps toward eliminating most of the factors we already know are responsible for most crime. It is the same kind of culture we need for a more peaceful world. How we might create that culture is the subject to which we now turn.

8

New Culture, Less Victimization

A nation that cannot get angry at its official betrayers has lost a resource
more important than any [other].

Garry Wills

Victims Still

DESPITE the heyday of victim policy during the last dozen years, victimization has not declined, and victims are still victims. Victims are still fearful;
still robbed, brutalized, and murdered in numbers almost unprecedented else-
where around the world; still victimized in the criminal process; and still manipulated politically for official ends.

As we have seen, officials from the Reagan and Bush administrations on
down have done little to pursue new strategies to significantly reduce
victimization. Instead, they have only intensified the failed policies of the
past. The U.S. media have abetted these policies by failing to hold officials
accountable. The media have distracted us with sensationalism, diverting our
attention from crime's sources and the changes that could significantly reduce
victimization.

An impressive array of new victims' policies, while helping the few, have
produced little overall gains for victims, but they have increased official
powers. Victims' policies have been largely symbolic, promising significant
change while delivering little of any real consequence—including serious rights
protections for victims. Nevertheless, political rhetoric can be a powerful
force in rallying support for official policies, from civil rights rollbacks to
crime wars. Often empty victims' policies have coopted the mainstream

victims' movement, generating public support for administrations that have little real sympathy for victims—indeed, they have specialized in helping to create them both at home and abroad.

Mainstream law enforcement has met criminal violence with a massive barrage of official violence. We are not only a culture of violence, but also a culture of violent solutions. We launch wars to solve our problems—in foreign lands or in our own streets. Wars on crime and drugs seem impressive, but beyond failing, they help create more victims than ever before.

What do victims want? Officials claim they want more toughness, more violence, more revenge. Some do, but then, never hearing real alternatives and being subjected to an unending media and government call for more violence, how could victims think otherwise? Still, surprising numbers of victims do not: They want policies that really reduce victimization in the first place. Otherwise, many victims are far less interested in revenge; they are far more interested in influence, information, assistance, respect, remorse, and accountability—in one word, *responsiveness* (Pepinsky, 1991a).

Given the entrenchment of mainstream crime policy, where can victims turn? Most challenges to official approaches either incredibly call for still greater government violence an the one hand or superficially toy with procedural reforms on the other. Most of those in power have little incentive to significantly reduce victimization, because doing so would fundamentally challenge the system from which they derive their power and well-being.

Most other Americans have a big incentive for change, but few apparent means at their disposal. To significantly reduce victimization, we need the makings of a new American culture, with new means and new ends. It would be a culture that would produce not only less criminal victimization but also less general victimization. It would be a just rather than an unjust culture in which power, resources, and opportunities were equitably distributed—in practice, not merely in rhetoric. It would be a nonviolent rather than a violent culture in which problems were addressed not only seriously and aggressively, but also peacefully and in a manner that befits civilized human beings, not barbarians.

A More Peaceful Culture

Most analyses passing as criminal-justice critiques at best provide only superficial diagnoses and modest reforms. They tell us we need new patrol strategies, tougher judges, or better information systems. These proposals merely tinker with U.S. crime policy, leaving it largely intact.

Societies constantly change. Rapid transformations around the world in the past couple of years, however, have dramatically escalated the pace of change. The *idea* of change has captured the public imagination. Although it is tempting to think we have "won" and can go our merry way, many Americans realize that we are not unlike citizens of the former Soviet Union and Eastern Europeans in having deep-seated problems. If they can open themselves for self-analysis and change, then why should the United States not have its own *glasnost* and *perestroika*?

Crime and violence linger as two of the United States' most serious problems, and yet conventional solutions have failed. Critics of mainstream policy, however, have provided few specific alternatives (Harvey, 1988; Wishnu, 1989), thus ceding the "crime issue" to society's most conservative forces. In this time of change, having real alternatives to combat these and other social problems would be more compelling than ever. Radical criminology must begin taking victims seriously, and a radical victimology must undo the co-optation the victims' movement has thus far largely suffered (McShane & Williams, 1992; Phipps, 1986; Rafter, 1987; Taylor, 1981).

An alternative strategy would neither assume official benevolence nor perpetuate conventional law-and-order strategies; it would propose neither superficial liberal nor conservative reforms. It would not recount, however real, the horrors of criminal victimization or the second victimization that victims face in the criminal process. It would not lament the protection of defendants' rights to the detriment of victims' rights. It would dwell on neither victims' assistance and recovery nor individual strategies for self-protection. It would not blame crime on victims, offenders, or criminal-justice institutions. By examining the crime problem narrowly, it would not be politically safe. It would not perpetuate top-down, official solutions that co-opt victim movements and citizen action. It would not analyze the crime problem piecemeal or apart from contemporary social conditions. And it would not critique conventional crime policy while neglecting concrete alternatives. These are among the reasons why mainstream crime policy repeatedly fails.

Any serious victims' policy must necessarily be linked to a broader, fundamentally different anticrime policy. We need a new, "get-smart" crime-control strategy that rejects outdated cliches that hold war and violence as the only ways to get "serious" about crime. People want peaceful communities: Only justice can produce that peace, but only peaceful, nonviolent means can produce justice—including criminal justice. Rather than being utopian, active nonviolence may be the only realistic way of reducing crime and victimization. Such an approach would promote victims as actors, not pawns; equal laws for all; and crime control, not social control

Victims as Actors, Not Pawns

Victims and their advocates must demand fundamental changes in criminal justice and in the United States' social institutions. Victims must avoid being political and administrative pawns, and the victims' movement must avoid being politically manipulated. Tinkering with criminal justice must give way to substantial reforms that give victims power rather than only formal rights.

Making victims into political actors rather than pawns requires a new victims' movement, a human rights strategy, new victims' services, and selective cooperation.

A New Victims' Movement

We need an active and independent, rather than a passive and official (that is, government-sponsored), victims' movement that encompasses the feminist, human rights, anticorporate, abolitionist, and other victims' movements. Passively relying on unmotivated, if not unsympathetic, officials to enforce victims' rights within a system that is rigged against their effective protection is no substitute for our actively demanding that social and crime policies seriously address victimization at its source. Rather than co-optation and symbolic change, victims need real power and a genuinely revitalized society.

A Human Rights Strategy

Crime victims now pursue a piecemeal rights competition against offenders—a zero-sum game in which one group's well-being relies on the other's misery. Instead, crime victims should embrace a human rights strategy that recognizes victimization's cultural sources, which are often ignored or fomented by the very elites upon whom victims now so often rely for protection. Most offenders commit crimes in response to social decay and official neglect: Although criminals indeed victimize others, they themselves also have been victimized. They will stop victimizing only when they, too, escape victimization.

A human rights analysis recognizes the connection between social victimization and criminal victimization (as suggested, for example, in the U.N. Declaration on the Victims of Crime and the Abuses of Power (Lamborn, 1987a; United Nations Secretariat, 1980). Such an analysis stresses the importance of both substantive and procedural rights for victims, offenders, and other citizens alike. Seriously enforcing human rights by curbing abuses of power would remove the social, political, and economic repressions that generate most crime, thus producing fewer victims and less victimization (Fattah, 1989, 1992c). The United States should be pressured into implementing this declaration and all of the other U.N. human rights covenants (Bassiouni, 1985; DeCataldo Neuberger, 1985; Eide, 1986; Fattah, 1989; Hertzberg, 1981; Johnston, 1974, 1978; Kim, 1983; Lopez-Rey, 1985; Lynch, McDowall, & Newman, 1988; Schaaf, 1986).

New Victims' Services

We need victims' services that really serve victims' needs, not official needs, and that stress victimization's psychological effects in particular. Feminist and other services that challenge the social conditions that generate victimization must be elevated over official services that are designed to enlist victims into status quo crime-control strategies and political campaigns. Rather than vengeance and participation, victims need to feel that they are informed about, supported in, and influential over their case. Federally sponsored victim compensation should also be available in every state to promptly repay—without exception—every victim of violent crime. A reconciliation and forgiveness model of victim involvement should replace the revenge model.

Selective Cooperation

Victims should not be swept up in official strategies for controlling crime and participating in the criminal process. They should resist harmful and counterproductive mainstream crime policies. Instead, victims should cooperate selectively and only with law-enforcement agencies that adopt alternative policies that really help rather than co-opt crime victims (Elias, 1982).

Equal Laws for All

There are limits to the change the legal system can produce. The law cannot stop crime. In particular, using the law to impose draconian punishments will not prevent victimization; our already stringent penalties are counterproductive. Nevertheless, the law can make some important adjustments in how we approach the crime problem. It can productively refocus law-enforcement energies and eliminate discriminatory double standards, thus reconstructing criminal law according to the real harm that crime causes to others.

Generating equal and productive laws for all of us requires decriminalization, depenalization, criminalization, and gun control.

Decriminalization

We should decriminalize drug use and possession, end our counterproductive drug wars, divert law-enforcement personnel to more serious problems, and thereby eliminate the extensive crime and violence that drug criminalization has generated (Nadelman, 1992; Reiman, 1984). Drug abuse should be addressed instead through treatment, education, and social revitalization (Chambliss, 1988; Currie, 1989). Likewise, gambling, prostitution, homosexuality, and other victimless crimes also should be decriminalized.

Depenalization

Criminal penalties should be reevaluated and reduced. Imprisonment does not achieve its penological objectives; it generates more crime instead. Incarceration should be mandated only as a last resort, and more effective prison alternatives should instead be incorporated into the criminal law (Box-Grainger, 1986; Currie, 1985; Flicker, 1990).

Criminalization

Punishment should fit the harm, not the person (Reiman, 1984). Corporate, white-collar, and government wrongdoing such as Wall Street stock fraud, the Exxon Valdez oil spill, and the savings-and-loan, Iran-Contra, and HUD scandals have produced far more damage, loss, and injury than have common crimes. These harms should be incorporated into the criminal law and sanctioned proportionally to their impact (Moore & Mills, 1990). Penal inequities between common crimes and corporate, white-collar, and government offenses should be eliminated.

Gun Control

The proliferation of guns in U.S. society promotes crime, violence, and accidents. Comprehensive and stringent gun-control laws should be adopted nationally and in every state to prevent new sales and to begin eliminating the millions of guns already distributed (Grassi, 1991; Reiman, 1984). Arms control is as important to domestic peace as it is to world peace.

Crime Control, Not Social Control

Law enforcement now devotes overwhelming resources to largely fruitless anticrime crusades that increase rather than decrease victimization. The enforcement of drug and other victimless crimes dominates police work. Enforcement double standards turn crime control into the social control of largely poor and minority communities. Instead, the criminal process must be reoriented. We must assess the limits of what enforcement can achieve and refocus it equitably on the most serious victimization. Reorienting criminal-justice priorities can help relieve overloaded courtrooms and overworked officials, a combination that so often produces injustice for both victims and criminals.

Pursuing serious crime control rather than social control requires a cultural strategy; peace, not war; problem-oriented policing; diversion; and equal rights.

A Cultural Strategy

Crime does not come from inherently evil offenders, lax enforcement, or careless victims. Rather, most crime comes from social and cultural decay; only serious social change can stop it. Thus, law enforcers cannot prevent crime; we must abandon our unrealistic expectations about police work. To the limited extent that it can, the criminal process should address the causes of crime rather than merely unleash state power against its symptoms. Because police officers are themselves often victims of conventional notions of law and order (Elias 1993c), they have an additional incentive to help promote the cultural change that is needed to reduce victimization.

Peace, Not War

We must end our futile crime and drug wars. We should replace the war metaphor with a peace metaphor and launch a peace movement against crime and its cultural sources (Quinney & Wildeman, 1991). We should pursue a more feminist justice that focuses less on how to end crime and more on how to achieve greater social harmony—not with utopianism, but with hardheaded strategies (Messerschmidt, 1986). We should move from a rights-and-control model of justice based on hierarchy, conflict, power, and dehumanization to a care-and-response model based on equality, conflict resolution, mutuality, and empathy (Harris, 1991). Instead of asking how effective our programs are in controlling people and crime, we should be trying to find out what is so lacking in the lives of our neighbors that they see no alternative but a life of crime and violence (Quinney & Wildeman, 1991).

Problem-Oriented Policing

Crime may result from social disorder, but aggressive order maintenance by police makes matters worse. Criminals are often victims, too—products of failed public policies. Our response should be to heal, not enforce (Skogan, 1990). We must reconstitute police work as community service rather than as community control. We should redesign the policing role to encourage law-enforcement agencies to change rather than to preserve the conditions that breed crime. Because crime is a social problem, police should work in communities to address its sources. They should not merely react to crime but should instead help communities organize themselves to prevent crime by developing social programs rather than merely protective gadgets and strategies (Quinney & Wildeman, 1991).

Law-enforcement funding must be redistributed to these programs to help youths, families, and the disadvantaged (Glasser, 1991). Law enforcers must practice minimal policing and be entirely accountable (beyond mere civilian review) to communities rather than to political or bureaucratic hierarchies. Police agencies should practice minimal intervention, pursuing serious investigation and detection (especially in neglected areas such as domestic violence) rather than surveillance and control (Kinsey, Lea, & Young, 1986). Police departments should use minimal coercion and shun grandiose control schemes. State power should be reduced, not enhanced (Messerschmidt, 1986); police forces should be demilitarized (if not eventually disarmed); and bans on police violence must be strictly enforced (Hutchinson, 1990b).

Diversion

Decriminalization and informal alternatives, such as mediation, treatment, and community conflict resolution, would significantly reduce and divert the cases that now preoccupy criminal-justice agencies from police departments to prisons. Diversion would double the time that law-enforcement agencies have available to help prevent other, more serious crimes. Diversion would reduce police crime, corruption, and brutality; reduce courtroom overloads; and reduce victim abuses in the criminal process.

Equal Rights

Police officers do not deserve the blame they often feel they get for not stopping crime. To avoid blame and to try to increase their effectiveness (however illusionary), they routinely cut corners. Although they are responsible for enforcing the law, in practice they often break (by committing their own crimes) or bend (by violating other people's rights) the law, undermining their own and others' respect for the law. To fight crime, our so-called law-and-order policy violates the rights of suspects, defendants, and the public; it victimizes while purportedly seeking to end victimization. Viewing crime as a social problem, however, can help lift the responsibility for crime from law enforcers' shoulders. Under these circumstances, police officers could begin to see rights (for offenders, victims, and other citizens alike) not as impediments, but as the most effective vehicles for their own professionalization and for reducing crime—by eliminating the human rights injustices that cause most crime (Glasser, 1991; Siegel, 1989; Walker, 1982).

Beyond rights protections, law-enforcement institutions (throughout the system) must apply their power equitably to overcome a legacy of discrimination against women, minorities, and the disadvantaged. Helped by more equitable criminal laws and thus freed from old double standards, officials must be held accountable for equal enforcement, arrest, charging, counseling, prosecution, conviction, sentencing, and punishment (Reiman, 1984).

Ending Male Violence

Women who are criminally victimized do not just *happen* to be women. They are victimized *because* they are women; in this sense, almost all crimes against women are "hate" crimes. Piecemeal reforms cannot solve the problem of women's systematic victimization. We can only do so by taking steps to eliminate sexism and patriarchy in U.S. society.

Some aspects of how we can achieve that objective are clear; it is more a matter of political will and power. But other challenges in the elimination of sexism are far more troublesome and have led to serious rifts even among feminists as to the best strategy. Some argue for strict new criminal laws and penalties and for a new enhancement of state power; they offer persuasive arguments in their justifiable outrage against the epidemic of violence against women in American society (Strauss, 1988).

Other feminists, however, question whether such strategies would only repeat previously failed get-tough strategies (toward other crimes); they also fear an enhancement of state power in the hands of overwhelmingly antifeminist officials. This is an area in which we might all agree as critics that we deplore the sources of violence against women and yet we differ on exactly the right solution. The following strategy pursues an approach that is consistent with the development of our critique of the law-and-order approach.

An antiviolence strategy requires a balance of legal and social policies. Legal reforms have their place, but only deeper cultural change will eliminate the conditions that routinely generate violence against women. Ending male violence requires gender democracy, serious enforcement, strategic punishment, and a nonsexist culture.

Gender Democracy

We need real political, economic, and social democracy to end the inequalities that oppress women and children and subject them both to institutional victimization and attacks by men. For example, women's economic dependence often traps them in violent households; an alternative public policy would ensure that they have the economic means to escape. The family, and not merely society, must be genuinely democratized (Hutchings, 1988; Messerschmidt, 1986). Accordingly, we also need an alternative socialization in our schools and other institutions to counter sexism and eliminate the values and behaviors of machismo, violence, and dominance, thereby withdrawing the tacit social permission to victimize women that men have been given by our culture (Faludi, 1991).

Serious Enforcement

We need feminist crime statistics to draw attention to the real level of violence against women (Radford & Stanko, 1991). We need serious law enforcement against domestic violence and sexual assault. The home, for example, should not remain a sanctuary for violence under the guise of protecting privacy; men should no longer be viewed as "kings of their castle." Women should not have to adapt to violence while the system and culture remain the same. We need to prevent the co-optation of feminist perspectives to serve patriarchal and law-and-order objectives. Some initiatives that purportedly support women have instead merely put them in weak and defenseless positions (thereby undermining their autonomy) in which male officials act as protectors; all the while ignoring the continuing sexism that produces the violence in the first place (Radford & Stanko, 1991).

Rape laws and prosecutions should put the accused, not women, on trial. This need not prevent a defendant from receiving a fair trial (James, 1992). The impediments to routine convictions for sexual assaults should be eliminated. Trials should inquire into a man's blameworthiness, not a woman's; and nonconsent should be credited (and convictions should be reached) not just when men use force, but also when they should have reasonably known that they were not given permission (Estrich, 1987).[1]

In addition, black solidarity should not prevent black men from being rightfully convicted of sexually assaulting black women (Morgan, 1992). The prosecution of black men, however, should not cover up a mainstream political agenda that is more concerned with imprisoning black men than with protecting black women (Mama, 1989). There should be significant increases in women police officers and other personnel to reduce police brutality and to increase official sensitivity to male violence and female victimization both inside and outside the home. Finally, we need significant new funding and support for progressive programs to help abusive men (Storrie & Poon, 1991) and to assist rape crisis and family violence centers provide better help to women *and* challenge conventional social and crime-control strategies (Radford & Stanko, 1991).

Strategic Punishment

We cannot excuse male violence simply because most of it results from sexism and capitalist patriarchy; we must take short-term measures against this violence and hold guilty men responsible, even while we work to resolve its causes (Delacoste & Newman, 1981; Kelly & Radford, 1987; Smith, 1986). Nevertheless, our draconian penalties (the toughest in the world), which we use for so many other crimes, do not work. We have no reason to believe they would magically begin to work against men who commit violence against women—no matter how justifiably outraged we are at the situation.

Instead, we need strategic punishments. The sureness of punishment (that is, routine convictions) and availability of real treatment reduce violence better than long-term incarceration (Box-Grainger, 1986). Mid-range penalties will make convictions more likely and effective (Kelly & Radford, 1987; Mama, 1989; Smart, 1989). We must recognize male violence such as rape as an odious crime and give top priority to eliminating it from our society. Short mandatory sentences that include a rigorous treatment program should be given to all first-time rapists. Longer mandatory sentences with more treatment (for those who were not treated effectively the first time) should be given to repeat offenders but routinely reviewed, with parole possible when the sentence has been completed under professional supervision (Box-Grainger, 1986).

Get-tough sentencing is a double-edged sword: It is important to treat battering and sexual assault seriously, but the enforcers are overwhelmingly sexist men just like the batterers. Harsh punishments give more power to men and the police, courts, and state that they control (Brants & Koh, 1986). As with other crimes, the law-and-order approach ignores the underlying causes of this violence (Hanmer, Radford, & Stanko, 1989). The get-tough punishments favored by some feminists (as well as by conservative officials who detest feminism) vastly overestimate the ability of sentencing to create social change. The criminal law cannot end male violence any more than it can end capitalist exploitation; victimizers should be held accountable, but social change requires much more than the criminal law.

Harsher penalties for rape, for example, will not reduce sexual assault because harshness does not deter (it more likely reinforces the behavior) or effectively incapacitate: As long as we have a sexist society, those who could be imprisoned—even through an overwhelming crusade—will be only a fraction of the potential or actual rapists out in society (Box-Grainger, 1986; Caringella-MacDonald & Humphries, 1991). Aside from being a flagrant rights violation and stock reactionary strategy, preventive incapacitation will not work: We cannot predict who will or will not rape or batter. Proposals to eliminate the "degrees" of sexual assault—while trying to show greater seriousness about the problem—are more likely to deter prosecution and conviction out of fear that punishment might be inappropriately severe (Box-Grainger, 1986).

Seeking revenge through harsh penalties contradicts basic feminist philosophy, which embraces nonviolent rather than violent solutions for social problems (Harris, 1991). Feminism is more in line with the abolitionist approach, where punishment is scaled back in deference to more nonviolent community (not state) alternatives (Knopp, 1991).

Nonsexist Culture

Pornography and prostitution, variously defined, can seriously harm women. Even short of direct harm—such as the violence, for example, that might be induced by viewing a pornographic movie—we should deplore depictions or actions that show the degradation or violation of women. First Amendment arguments that suggest that free speech requirements should prevent *any* restrictions on pornography are misguided. We might lament, in many ways, that free expression has not been protected more universally by the courts over the years; but pornography is the wrong place to begin rectifying that wrong. Free expression must be balanced against other social ends. In a nonsexist society, restrictions on pornography might be unnecessary. Until then, the problem cannot simply be ignored.

On the other hand, we face the danger of imposing restrictions that are as counterproductive as draconian punishments are for other crimes. We should be wary of repressive laws—even those proposed by some feminists—that really promote reactionary agendas under the guise of eliminating prostitution and pornography (Pepinsky, 1991a). Antipornography crusades, which are often supported by society's most repressive forces (such as Ed Meese, Jesse Helms, and their ilk), probably will not help women and would instead promote a law-and-order agenda that increases rather than decreases male privilege (Valverde, 1985). Elements of some prostitution and pornography might lead to greater violence against women and children. Unfortunately, criminalizing prostitutes and pornographers attacks only the symptoms of the problem, not the cause. Many feminists concerned about male violence nevertheless argue against criminalization as the solution (Ehrenreich, 1990; Messerschmidt, 1986; Smart, 1989; Willis, 1984).[2]

What is *pornography?* Unless we have a commonly accepted definition, how do we know where to draw the line, and how can we trust the sexist male establishment that would be enforcing laws based on these definitions? Unfortunately, we cannot agree on what constitutes pornography. Some people believe that nothing is pornographic and that everything goes. Others believe that it is any representation that is intended to arouse sexual desire. Other people want to distinguish pornography from erotica. Still others believe that pornography is what portrays violence against women (ranging from insults to degradation and direct physical violence). Others believe that pornography is anything that causes violence against women.

Some critics believe that advertising, mainstream media, beauty standards, beauty contests, and even romance novels are pornographic. Others believe that sex education, AIDS information, sexual freedom, abstract or unconventional art, sexually suggestive novels, abortion and birth-control information, and even the Equal Rights Amendment are pornographic, and they would love to use antipornography laws to censor them. And still other critics—including some feminists—believe that men are inherently violent and that heterosexuality, by definition, constitutes violence against women.[3] Ironically, in the hands of right-wing administrators, the antipornography laws proposed by these feminists could easily be used against them, their life-styles, and those of other sexual minorities; do these advocates really want laws advocated in the past by the likes of J. Edgar Hoover (Rubin, 1984; Valverde, 1985)?

So how do we impose a cure that is not worse than the disease? We should first focus on those fundamental sources of violence: We need cultural change that will help end the sexist society that produces the worst abuses of sexually explicit media. This requires not only institutional change, but also alternative forms of education and socialization. Next, we need to empower women generally rather than subject them to the whims of male power. We should equalize responsibility for the behavior we are trying to discourage: Both prostitutes and the men who use them should be equally stigmatized.

We must take political action against the most exploitative representations of women, which range from advertisements to fashion to sexually explicit films. Men and women alike should also challenge the men in our lives to undo their sexist attitudes and behaviors (Rubin, 1984; Smart, 1989; Valverde, 1985). Finally and most important, people who produce sexist materials must be held accountable for specific harms they cause. In other words, they should be held at least financially liable in civil tort proceedings where actual harm (from a pornographic movie, for example) can be proven. Financial incentives can act as a more effective deterrent to pornographers than criminal penalties, and they may be a more effective stop-gap measure on the way toward a less sexist society.

Less Punishment Is More

Conventional crime policy promotes harsh criminal punishments, which are ineffective, repressive, and even counterproductive: We have both the world's highest incarceration rate and one of the world's highest crime rates. Harsh penalties achieve no legitimate correctional goals: They do not deter, reform, treat, or rehabilitate. Most prisoners initially are not a threat to society, but they become increasingly dangerous the longer they are imprisoned. Building more prisons does not stop crime, it only warehouses increasing numbers of outcasts from American culture.

Instead, a productive correctional strategy requires equity, decarceration, and prisoners' rights.

Equity

Through decriminalization, we need to eliminate many vice crimes whose perpetrators now clog our nation's prisons. These "crimes" should be handled through treatment and education. Penalties should be reduced for the remaining serious common crimes. Shorter punishment that is more surely and equally administered will be more effective than draconian punishment. As a matter of equity, corporate, white-collar, and government crimes should not be excused but should be punished like common crimes, proportional to the harm done.

Decarceration

While establishing more equitable criminal penalties and a more responsive society (that is, one that is accountable for crime's sources) (Pepinsky, 1991a), we should significantly reduce the use of prisons as punishment, thus reducing the crime generated by the institutions' own violence (Knopp, 1976). We should close prisons and slash prison populations, most of which even hardened wardens claim are no violent threat to society. While aiming toward eliminating most prisons (de Haan, 1990, 1991), reduced imprisonment should be accompanied by a new upsurge in correctional alternatives such as restitution, mediation, training, reconciliation, work release, conflict resolution, community service, and psychological and other counseling (Dittenhoffer & Ericson, 1992; Martino, 1991; Quinney & Wildeman, 1991). Supervised parole and probation should be restored as workable options, freed from discrimination and other injustices.

For our current punitive model, we should substitute a treatment or social change model of corrections (Currie, 1985; Quinney & Wildeman, 1991). We need a kind of social rehabilitation that links individual change to social change —that is, individual rehabilitation not simply by adapting to society but rather by changing the social conditions of that society (Currie, 1985; MacLennan, 1992). And we should restore the role of victim-offender interactions in resolving criminal conflicts (Christie, 1982).

Prisoners' Rights

For those who remain in prison, the experience should be made productive; otherwise, more rather than less crime will result. This can be achieved not merely by the right treatment and programs, but also by taking seriously prisoner's rights, especially as they affect prison conditions and discipline. All prisons should be required to exceed the United Nations' minimum standards. There must be minimum educational standards for prison guards. Prisoners must be given widespread privileges to help them develop responsible life-styles. Their citizenship rights should be preserved as much as possible; so should their connections to whatever community ties they may once have had. Finally, the death penalty—a fundamental human rights violation—should be universally abolished.

Community Justice

Conventional crime policy emphasizes individuals as the source of crime. It rallies communities against criminals. Government-sponsored community crime-prevention stresses police strategies, target-hardening hardware, neighborhood suspiciousness, and official control. Yet neighborhood watches and other government-inspired strategies have little effect on crime because they largely ignore crime's deeper sources in U.S. communities (Carriere & Ericson, 1989; Barr & Pease, 1990). As strategies fail, vigilantism increases.

Rather than restrictive *social* control, we need more democratic *public* control—community revitalization and social change directed by residents and not co-opted by officials. We need community crime control focused not on building armed fortresses but on analyzing the fundamental sources of conflict: violence and crime in our neighborhoods, a more nonviolent enforcement focused on community problem solving (Tifft & Sullivan, 1980).

An independent, community justice requires community assessment, community strategies, community culture, and community politics.

Community Assessment

We need to focus on community conditions as the source of crime and pursue strategies that allow residents to take back their communities from counterproductive political and economic institutions. Beyond self-defense mechanisms, what are the internal and external causes of neighborhood crime? We should assess what conditions in each community produce antisocial behavior, including unemployment, drug use, poor education, racial tensions, youth problems, declining local resources, and inadequate political power.

Community Strategies

Based on our community diagnosis of crime, we need cooperative planning to recapture local control over political and economic decisions. We should plan short- and long-term strategies to deal with current crime while planning ways to prevent future crime. We need to organize so that we can demand the resources needed to address the root causes of crime and other community problems (Marable, 1989). Community organizations are more effective than law-enforcement agencies in promoting the kind of order that reduces crime (Currie, 1985; Skogan, 1990). Thus, we should rely more on our own groups, such as community protection councils (Hutchinson, 1990b), and rely less on formal government bureaucracies (Michalowski, 1985). We should promote neighborhood cooperation and integration, not distrust and competition. Rather than blind obedience to police directives, which often lead to co-optation, communities must tell law enforcers what they need, based on their own evaluation of their community's problems. Official stereotypes about effective crime control should be challenged and abandoned.

Community Culture

Taking local control over the crime problem can perhaps help communities rediscover themselves, thus rejuvenating or inventing new community cultures. Because community justice requires a broad assessment of neighborhood conditions rather than artificially isolating the crime problem, communities could use the opportunity to help clarify and define what they stand for, including what values they represent. This can produce healthier, less atomized, and more cooperative communities, which are less conducive to crime, violence, and conflict. Organized, cooperative, and politically active communities are less crime-ridden (Hutchinson, 1990b).

Community Politics

To get some adequate response to its own assessment of its needs, communities must develop an effective politics. In other words, communities must learn how to get and exercise power. With that power they should establish local justice institutions that respond more directly (than distant or outsider bureaucracies) to individual communities. These include programs for police review, mediation and dispute resolution, community policing and corrections, rape crisis and domestic violence, and community drug needs (Bass, 1992). Communities should explicitly reject vigilantism (and challenge the accountability of groups such as the Guardian Angels) and recognize how crime and violence can inappropriately escalate racial and class tensions (Klein, Luxenburg, & Gunther, 1991). Communities should say no to conventional political responses that suggest that crime is inevitable or vulnerable only to isolated, get-tough solutions. Instead, a revitalized citizen politics could convince people that we *can* fight city hall, reduce crime, solve our community's problems, and have some control over our own lives.

Social Justice

Mainstream crime control reflects and reinforces contemporary American culture. It ignores the social injustices underlying most crime, and it blocks the social change most needed to eliminate those injustices. A culture that celebrates violence and generates widespread powerlessness and despair can only produce a cycle of violence met by violent official responses. If we do not move toward a new culture, then rampant crime and violence will continue.

We can have a less violent culture only by addressing the roots of American crime, which are deeply embedded in our political and economic institutions. Those institutions create adverse social conditions that violate people's human rights. They foster conditions that breed most crime. Taking human rights seriously requires not only a more just legal system and a less criminal government, but also basic changes in the U.S. system—particularly in corporate-state capitalism. Like the former Soviet Union, the United States also needs a kind of *glasnost* and *perestroika*.

Achieving the social justice needed to reduce crime requires economic democracy, political democracy, and a democratic culture.

Economic Democracy

We need structural changes that would democratize both the process and outcomes of the United States' economic system. We need serious policy reforms to overcome the problems that cause crime, such as poverty, inequality, unemployment, racism and sexism, broken families, and community disintegration. Economic democracy requires a comprehensive social insurance scheme (one similar to European models) for all Americans, and it should include approaches such as workplace democracy, public ownership, industrial cooperatives, family care, full employment and job training, universal shelter and nutrition, equal educational opportunity, minimum guaranteed standards of living, public control of investment, national health care, demilitarization, and real antitrust enforcement (Nader, 1992). Corporate harms should be criminalized like common crimes, and corporate power must be severely curtailed. We should end cutthroat economic competition and reduce American materialism and individualism (Hutchinson, 1990b; Messerschmidt, 1986; Michalowski, 1985).

We should pay particular attention to young people, investing in preventive programs (against drugs and delinquency) for juveniles and rehabilitation schemes that are supported well enough to give them a fighting chance (Currie, 1991). We need a progressive family policy, including birth planning, support, child care, day care, and educational reform (Currie, 1985). We should develop public-sector employment programs and local economic development schemes, not misguided, private-sector urban enterprise zones (Currie, 1985). Finally, we must replace our war economy with a peace economy (Elias & Turpin, 1992).

Political Democracy

Obstacles to real political democracy undermine people's power, rights, and control, which in turn produce alienation, powerlessness, and then crime committed by people both inside and outside formal government. We need political democracy both in political outcomes and in political decision-making power. It requires real (not merely formal) equality, human rights, participation, choice, decentralization, and community control. Political empowerment will make crime a less attractive alternative and give people more power to control crime in their own communities.

Democratic Culture

To achieve and sustain political and economic democracy, we need a more democratic culture. We must promote alternative social values in our education, media, and other socializing institutions. These values should reflect the aforementioned structural changes and include sharing, nonviolence, public service, cooperation, community, racial and sexual equality, and human dignity and human rights.

Better Thinking About Crime

The prevailing thinking about crime in United States assumes that crime is inevitable, that it is committed by irretrievably evil people, and that nothing much can be done about it short of get-tough measures to hold the line against society's worst violence (Wilson, 1975; Wilson & Herrnstein, 1985). As we have suggested herein, this is a needlessly pessimistic view, ripe for exploitation by the society's most reactionary forces. We need better thinking about crime than this.

Unfortunately, this view pervades American society. It is strongly connected to our general world view of people who are "out to get us" and who only understand toughness and force. This assumption runs deep in the U.S. media, in government agencies (and certainly in the criminal process), in our educational system, and even in the ranks of academic professionals in criminology and victimology—who should know better. These self-defeating views, which prevent a serious approach to eliminating victimization and subject victims to symbolic gestures without much substance, are motivated both by politics and philosophy. Both must change. We need a progressive politics that brings out the best in people and a philosophy that sees the good side of human nature, not merely the bad. And we need cultural mechanisms— that is, means of developing new attitudes—that view the social problem of crime the same way as we view the technical problem of something as complicated as putting a person on the moon. We have to approach the problem seriously and positively.

Better thinking about crime and victimization requires a radical criminology and victimology and democratic socialization.

A Radical Criminology and Victimology

The recent Seville Statement on Violence, signed by many of the world's leading researchers, concludes that humans are not inherently violent; violence results from social conditions (Marullo & Hlavacek, 1992). Thus, we need not only a policy but also professional thinking that takes those conditions seriously. We need a more radical criminology that distinguishes itself from official perspectives, and which calls for the kind of fundamental changes in American culture that are needed to seriously reduce crime and victimization. And we need a more radical victimology that avoids official co-optation, promotes less symbolic and more substantive victim policies, recognizes the interdependence of criminal and social victimization, and calls for a serious reduction of victimization of all kinds (Fattah, 1992a, 1992b; Kelly & Radford, 1987). And we should further develop the notion of "criminology as peacemaking" as a way of bringing criminology and victimology closer together (Pepinsky & Quinney, 1989; Quinney & Wildeman, 1991; Snider, 1988). These are perspectives that should be more widely embraced by both academics and practitioners of criminal justice and victim services.

Democratic Socialization

When academics peer out of the ivory tower, they should challenge official perspectives rather than merely accept them (Barak, 1988). But broader forces of socialization in society also must embrace new thinking about crime if the public is ever expected to change its views on what causes crime and what can be done about it. Crime has long been an issue dominated by the political right. Political progressives must begin taking the issue back, providing new hope and new solutions that do not repeat the failed policies of either liberals or conservatives (McShane & Williams, 1992; Phipps, 1986). To do this publicly, we must challenge the media generally and challenge their crime coverage in particular; media activists have already begun this fundamental task (Solomon & Lee, 1991). Finally, we must educate people differently about the causes of crime and violence in our society. And we must educate generally to develop values other than competition, individualism, aggressiveness, private status, material accumulation, and mindless consumption—values not unrelated to the causes of crime and violence in American society.

Less Victimization

Taking crime seriously is a tall order, but short of working directly on the causes of victimization, crime victims will gain little from the piecemeal reforms that have been adopted thus far. While the alternatives proposed herein face serious political obstacles, they nevertheless provide a new strategy that is unlikely to fail as miserably as official programs have thus far; indeed, it is a strategy that could succeed against crime and also help undo various other kinds of victimization in American society. These proposals also may shake us from the debilitating assumption that we can do nothing other than what we have always done; it is the least we owe crime victims old and new. A new victim movement, embracing these strategies, could unite the crime victim movement with other, more marginalized victim movements and begin pursuing a new victimology of human rights.

Notes

1. Stop means stop, not go, in this day and age; even a man's honest view that consent was given or implied does not eliminate guilt if he drew that conclusion unreasonably (that is, after being told to stop). If social pressures sometimes push women to say yes when they mean no, then the least we can do is protect those who take the risk and say no (Estrich, 1987).

2. Some critics argue that antipornography crusaders use unrepresentative child pornography and so-called slasher pornography to push a simplistic solution for a complex problem (Rubin, 1984). Some believe the crusades play on cliches of female innocence and nurturing that desexualizes women and denies them pleasure and lust and other benefits of the sexual liberation movement of the 1960s and 1970s (Valverde, 1985). Still other critics believe that legal restrictions will further exploit women in the sex trade; it will drive prostitution and pornography production underground and into even worse conditions. Some see this as a middle-class feminism subverting lower-class women without providing them real alternatives to their sexual labors; discouraging this work is one thing, criminalizing it is another (Smart, 1989).

Other theorists believe that sex laws are a kind of sexual apartheid, discriminating not between right and wrong but between weak and strong, poor and rich (Rubin, 1984). Still others find it risky to predict violent behavior from one kind of pornography or another; and some argue that even if pornography causes some violence, no evidence exists that those not exposed to pornography commit any fewer sex crimes than those who are (Rubin, 1984). Some argue that rather than promoting sexual diversity rather than discrimination, antipornographic feminism merely replaces monogamous heterosexuality with monogamous homosexuality (under the theory that all heterosexual sex amounts to violence against women). And still other theorists believe that it is not so much that sexism comes from the pornography industry as that sexism causes the industry. Why not emphasize, they say, the far more serious sources of sexism and violence in society: the family, the state, media, religion, education, socialization, psychiatry, unequal pay, child-raising practices, and job discrimination (Rubin, 1984).

3. Are we willing to live with the extremes of these definitions that would surely be imposed if we gave free reign to many of the recent antipornography ordinances? If separatist feminists ever gained power, would we accept their definition of pornography as all heterosexual relations, whether portrayed or acted out? Should we accept their biological explanations for male violence any more than we are willing to accept them from law-and-order advocates about criminals generally (Messerschmidt, 1986)? More to the point, do we want to accept the definitions of those who actually do hold power, who would define pornography as all that which falls outside a sexist, right-wing ideology?

Appendix

REPRESENTATIVE HEADLINES

The following headlines were used in crime stories found from 1956 through 1991 in the three main newsweeklies: *Newsweek*, *Time*, and *U.S. News & World Report*.

1991

U.S. News
The Men Who Created Crack

Newsweek
Are Cities Obsolete?
Video Vigilantes
Keeping Teens Off the Street
When a Drunk Driver Kills
Big Crimes, Small Cities
The War at Home: How to Battle Crime
These Clients Aren't Fools
A Boost for Brady
The Widening Drug War
Violence in Our Culture

Sex Crimes: Women on Trial
Remove That Blue Dot: Naming Names
L.A.'s Violent New Video

Time
Putting the Brakes on Crime
The Uses of Monsters
What Say Should Victims Have?
Mind Games With Monsters
Should This Woman Be Named?
Back to the Beat
At the End of Their Tether

1990

U.S. News
The Latest Capital Battle Cry
Kidnapping Drug Lords
The Drug Warriors' Blues
Drug War: Murder in a "Model" City
Law Enforcment: Bleak Indictment of Inner City
Law: Child-Abuse Trial That Left National Legacy
New Frontier in the War on Drugs

Newsweek
Arms Race on Hill Street
New York's Nightmare

A New Line Against Crime
The Mind of the Rapist
Still Shocking After a Year
Women Under Assault
The Walled Cities of L.A.
A New Era of Punishment
Shielding Rape Victims
A Frontal Assault on Drugs
Race and Hype in a Divided City
Short Lives, Bloody Deaths
A Failed Test Case: Washington's Drug War
A Dirty Drug Secret
Uncivil Liberties?

Risky Business
Adios to the Andean Strategy?
The Canadian Connection
The Fryers Club Convention
Women in Jail: Unequal Justice
Farrakhan's Mission: Fighting Drug War His
  Way

Time
A Losing Battle
Georgie Porgie Is a Bully
May the Force Be With You

Guilty, Guilty, Guilty
Death by Gun
Up From the Streets
Doing the Right Thing
Going Public With Rape
The Sheriff Strikes Back
Turning Victims Into Saints
The View From Behind Bars
The War That Will Not End
A Seaside Chat About Drugs
More and More, a Real War

1989

U.S. News
Personalized Penalties
The Politics of Hate
A Criminal Lack of Common Sense
Victims of Crime
Chipping Away at Civil Liberties
Meltdown in Our Cities
When the Guilty Go Free
Dead Zones
The Meanest Street in Washington
How Best to Heal a Shattered Child
Murder in the Safest Places

Newsweek
Far Beyond Indifference
Society Loves a Good Victim
Murder, They Broadcast
Cops Above, Crime Below
Why Justice Can't Be Done
TV's Crime Wave Gets Real
The Newest Drug War
Hardening Their Hearts
Cops: We're Losing the War
Murder Wave in the Capital
We Need Drastic Measures
A Tide of Drug Killing
Experiments in Boot Camp
On the Alert Against Crime
Now It's Bush's War
Children of the Underclass

On the Firing Line
Profits in a Risky Business
Anarchy in Colombia
Taking on the Legalizers

Time
Doing the Crime, Not the Time
Our Violent Kids
Teenagers and Sex Crimes
Our Bulging Prisons
Wilding in the Night
Crime and Responsibility
Beware of Paper Tigers
Have Weapons, Will Shoot
Noble Battle, Terrible Toll
Supply Side Scourge
A Plague Without Boundaries
Truce or Consequences?
A Threat to Freedom?
Fighting Back
On the Front Lines
Blandishments and Bombs
Going Too Far
Attacking the Source
A Loose Cannon's Parting Shot
Here Come the Pregnancy Police
Evicting the Drug Dealers
Wimp No More
The Chemical Connection

1988

U.S. News
Sex, Drugs and Death
The Black-on-Black Crime Plague
What Should Be Done
Watch Those Watchdogs
Meese's Confrontation Strategy
A Major Target: Porn Peddlers
Theft-Proofing Your Car
Ethnic Gangs and Organized Crime
Will Drug Dealers Feel the Noose?
Congress Dopes Out a Drug Bill
Drugs on Main Street
A Modest Proposal for Dealing With Drugs
What "Zero Tolerance" Really Adds Up To
Soldiers Can't Beat Smugglers
No More Token Drug War?
The New Drug Vigilantes
Inside America's Biggest Drug Bust
The Demand-Side Drug Fix
When Drug Enforcement Confronts Foreign
  Policy

Newsweek
No Furlough From Crime
Hour by Hour Crack
Getting Tough on Cocaine
Parsing the Sentences
Fighting Crime by the Rules
Is the War on Drugs Another Vietnam?
Helping the Cops and Jails

Where Cocaine Is King
Crime in the Cities: Drug Connection
Should Drugs Be Legal?
Drug Testing in the Dock
Drug Gangs: The Big Sweep
A Web of Crime Behind Bars
Is Grandma in a Drug Ring?
When Cops Act on a Hunch
Going After a Porn Czar
Marco Polo of Marijuana

Time
Slaughter in the Streets
"Bad" Women and Brutal Men
Racial Equality
Fraud, Fraud, Fraud
Fact vs. Fiction on "Reality TV"
Kids Who Sell Crack
A Bloody West Coast Story
Where the War Is Being Lost
Busting the Tac Squad
Criminals Just Say Yes
A Drug Kingpin Goes Free
Glass Houses and Getting Stoned
Riding the Drug Issue
Tears of Rage
Desperados
The Cash Cleaners
Crack Comes to the Nursery

1987

U.S. News
The Flames of Fear
High Cost of FBI's High-Tech Crime Wars
Kids, Crime and Punishment
The Public Fights Back
Teaching Convicts Real Street Smarts
Miami Vice: Sorting Good Guys From Bad
  Guys
Busting the Drug Testers

Newsweek
Prime-Time Crime War

In Detroit, Kids Kill Kids
L.A. Law: Gangs and Crack
Insider Trading's Victims
Doing Hard Time, Fairly
Urban Murders: On the Rise

Time
Home Is Where the Hurt Is
"Not Guilty"
Sexual Abuse or Abuse of Justice?
When the Date Turns Into Rape
Black vs. White in Howard Beach

1986

U.S. News
Stop Drugs at the Source
Making Sense of Alarms
When Tenants Take Over
How to Stop Crime the Brainy Way
A Crime Rise That Stumps the Experts
The Black Underclass
For Men in Streets: Hustle Without Heroism
Fighting Crime Before It Happens
Helping Molested Children
Back to Basics in Crime War
What Our Readers Have to Say [about crime]
Tips on How to Spot Counterfeit Goods
Is Nature to Blame for Careers of Crime?
Drug Education Gets an F
War on Drugs: More Than Short Term High?
Fighting the War on Drugs From Trenches
Drugs: Now Prime Time
American Drugs
U.S. Mission: Cut Off Drugs at Source

Newsweek
Inside America's Toughest Prison

Can We Stop the Smugglers?
Crack and Crime
The Assault on Campus Crime
Acquaintance Rape Comes into the Open

Time
Hollywood Tapes and Testimony
Today's Native Sons
The Rio Grande's Drug Corridor
An Inmate and a Gentleman
Seeing Justice Never Done
Young Crime, Old Punishment
Reporting the Drug Problem
Rolling out the Big Guns
The Enemy Within
America's Crusade
Battle Strategies
Crack Down
High Aims, Low Comedy
Striking at the Source
Crack
Battling the Enemy Within

1985

U.S. News
Flood of Drugs—Losing Battle
   In the Trenches With Cocaine Fighters
   At the Border: A Frustrating Struggle
U.S. Antidrug Forces Will Not Be Intimidated
Drug War Gets Even More Vicious
Street Crime: People Fight Back
Designer Drugs: Murder by Molecule
Crime Rates City By City
Genetic Traits Predispose Some to
   Criminality

Newsweek
Drug Wars: Murder in Mexico

A G-Man's Anger
Feeding America's Habit
Cocaine's Rock Houses
Has Mexico Matched up on Drugs: DEA
   Agents Say No
Rape and the Law

Time
Deadly Traffic on the Border
Fighting the Cocaine Wars
Are Criminals Born, Not Made?
Up in Arms Over Crime

1984

U.S. News
Bloody Streets: Only Hope Is to Escape
Wins & Losses in War vs. Drug Abuse
Why Dead on Arrival? [crime bill]

Newsweek
California's War Against Pot
Time
The Bust of the Century
War on the Cocaine Mafia

1983

U.S. News
Crime Victims Ask Their Day in Court
Crackdowns on Judges Who Go Astray
Why Crime's Rapid Rise May Be Over
    When Courts Go After Career Criminals
Crime and Its Victims: An Official Look

Newsweek
Crime and the Law
ROTC for the Nation's Cops?
Why Crime Is on the Decline
    Murder Capital USA

Time
Drug Nets: Stepping Up the Attack
Crashing on Cocaine
A Red Light for Scofflaws
Cure Worse Than Disease? Paraquat Spraying
Private Violence
Child Abuse: The Ultimate Betrayal
Wife Beating: The Silent Crime
Rape: The Sexual Weapon

1982

U.S. News
Feds vs. Drug Runners: Game Gets Trickier
U.S. Legal System: All Sides Want to Hide
    Truth
As Calls Mount for Crackdown on Crime
Crime Finally Takes A Pause
How U.S. Is Cracking Down on Drug
    Smugglers
Crime Casts Cloud over Nation's Playground
American Justice: ABCs of How It Really
    Works
    The Complex Minuet of Criminal Courts
    Crime & Punishment: It Seldom Works
    That Way
    Police Find Themselves in Double
    Squeeze
    The Prosecutor—in Fiction and in Fact

Jury System Not Perfect, but It Works
Corruption Is Still a Fact of Life
Get-Tough Approach Makes a Comeback
The Legal Logjam on Death Row
Prisons, The Gamut Is From Bad to Worse

Newsweek
Reagan's War on Drugs
To Catch a Career Criminal
Reagan's War on Crime
When the Police Blunder a Little

Time
A New and Deadly Menace
Expensive Time: Pay as You Go Criminal?
Why Justice System Fails: Inefficient Ways
    of Coping With a Handful of Savages
What Crime Does to the Victims
Running Pot Where It's Not as Hot

1981

U.S. News
Behind Violence: Failure to Get Tough
Abusing the Aged: The Unreported Crime
Toll of Violence: 1.3 Million
Why the Crackdown on Pot Smugglers
Violence in Big Cities—Behind the Surge
Burger: Americans Hostages to Crime
The Reagan Way of Dealing With Crime
Stings Score Success, but How Much
    Longer?
Marijuana: A U.S. Farm Crop That's Booming
Our Losing Battle Against Crime

What Reagan Would Do To Put Clamp on
    Crime
U.S. Crime—Surging Again
The Crime Package That Sparked Bitter
    Dispute

Newsweek
New Federal War on Drugs
The Plague of Violent Crime
    Angels and Other Guardians
    Lock 'Em Up—But Where?
The Chief Justice Takes on Crime

Time
The Curse of Violent Crime
    If It Happens to You
Why the Justice System Fails
What Crime Does to the Victims

1980

U.S. News
Lawbreakers Turn to Greener Pastures
    Citizens Fight Back
California's Farm Boom—in Marijuana
Corruption and Mayhem—Inside Look at
    Mafia
Drug Dealers Hustle While Officials Argue
New Flood of Heroin, Why It Hasn't Stopped
Fear Stalks the Streets
When Citizens Mobilize Against Crime

Newsweek
Punishments That Fit the Crime
Fear of Crime Haunts U.S.
When Can Tainted Evidence Be Used?
Making Convicts Pay Their Victims
Strict Views of the Law

1979

U.S. News
Should Judges Make Laws?
Tale of Three Cities: Violent Crime
Unwanted Import From Iran: Heroin
A Blueprint to Fight Crime

1978

U.S. News
Behind the Violence: Lives Without Meaning
Violence in America: Getting Worse?
Where Drug Smuggling Is a Way of Life
Is U.S. Becoming a Drug-Ridden Society?

1977

U.S. News
Why Violent Crime Is Now in Fashion
For Business: FBI Advice on Curbing Crime
New Strategy Against Drug Rings
As Crime in the U.S. Starts to Level Off
Step-Up in Fight on Crimes Against Elderly

Burger Takes Aim at Crime
Trouble in Paradise
    Life in the Drug Trade
    Lost in the Laundry
Blueprint for Fighting Crime

Heroin: Preparing for a New Invasion
How the IRS Abets Crime
Miami's Narcobucks
Time
Potshots at Headshots
Absolute War in Our Streets
The Menace of Any Shadow
Making the Crimes Fit the Times
A New and Deadly Menace
Between Rock and Hard Case: Courts for
    Repeat Offenders
Toward More Uniform Sentences: Despite
    Double Jeopardy, Prosecutors Can Appeal
    Light Sentences
To Shoot or Not to Shoot?

Time
Crime Stoppers: Citizens Get into the Act
In Arizona: Tracks in the Desert
At Issue: Crime and Punishment

White Fear, Black Crime
Time
Stopping Crime as a Career
Fitting Justice?
Is Plea Bargaining a Cop-Out?

Jobs Behind Bars: Boon to Prisoners and
    Taxpayers
Now It's a Wave of Thefts in Historical
    Documents
Stepped Up Drive to Make Punishment Fit
    Crime

Needed: A New Crime Code

Newsweek
Compromising on the Code

Time
Fixed Sentences Gain Favor
The New England Connection
Just Leave It to the States
The Sierra Madre's Amapola War

1976

U.S. News
Crime's Big Payoff
How U.S. Aims to Dry Up Heroin Supply
War on Career Criminals Starts to Show Results
Behind Trend to Go Easy on Victimless Crimes
Certainty of Punishment Best Deterrent to Crime
Why Criminals Go Free: Revolving Door Justice
Glimmers of Hope on Crime Front

Newsweek
Colombia: The Coke Trade
Fairer Sentences
The Mexican Connection
The Snake Pits

Time
Bagging Heroin
Crime and Punishment
The Price of Rape
Gaining in the Cities
Reconsidering Suspects' Rights

1975

U.S. News
New Epidemic of Crime—The Causes and Cures
After 200 Years, U.S. Readies 1st Criminal Law Code
The Attorney General Speaks Out
Return of the Hard-Drug Menace
Sharpest Spurt Ever in Violence, Theft
Spiraling Crime—How to Protect Yourself
What About the Victims of Crime?
War on Crime—By Fed-Up Citizens

Big Change in Prisons: Punish—Not Reform

Newsweek
How to Get Your Man
Crime: Ford's Hard Line
Rocky Mountain High

Time
The Crime Wave
    Portrait of a Gang Leader
    The Causes/What Can Be Done
    Views From Behind Bars
Crime Boom

1974

U.S. News
What the Police Need to Do a Better Job
Crime: A High Price Tag That Everybody Pays
The Losing Battle Against Crime in America
Saxbe Warns of Peril in Crime Spurt

What It Takes to Stop Rampant Crime
Crime Wave Defies All Efforts
Violent Crime on Rise Again
War Against Organized Crime Is Being Won
How U.S. Is Smashing Hard Drug Rings

1973

U.S. News
Crime's First Drop in 17 Years
Crime: Signs That the Worst Is Over

Nixon Maps All-Out Attack on Crime and Drugs
What's Happened to Morality in America?

The Death Penalty Gets a Big Push
A New Drive Against Killers of Police
Comeback of Violence in America

Newsweek
How to Tell Who Will Kill
Drug Alert

Time
Women Against Rape
Crime: On the Decline
Nixon's Hard Line
Fighting Crime: Debate Between Rhetoric
    and Reality
Grass Grows More Acceptable

1972

U.S. News
Big Gains in Drive to Cut Off Narcotics
'72 Progress in Fight to Limit Crime
New Progress in War on Drugs
Victory Soon in Fight Against Drug Traffic?
Gains and Setbacks in the War on Crime
Antitrust, Crime, Drugs . . .
Latest Turn in Treatment of Drug Addicts
A Turning Point in Fight Against Crime?
Courts Too Easy on Crime? Police Chiefs
    Speak Out
Winning the War Against Organized Crime
Why Is Crime Now a Worldwide Epidemic?
Rising Crime Rate—Now It's the Suburbs'
    Turn

Cutting Crime: How Nation's Capital Does It
Crime and the Courts: A Judge Speaks Out
Drug Abuse Now Epidemic: What's Being
    Done
Drive to Curb Hard Drugs Gets No.1 Priority

Newsweek
The U.S. Scores in the War on Drugs
Living With Crime, USA
To Save Our Cities
Heroin: Now It's the Latin Connection

Time
Search and Destroy: The War on Drugs
    Portrait of A Narc
Street Crime: Who's Winning?
    Portrait of A Mugger and His Turkeys

1971

U.S. News
Where War Against Crime Is Being Won
Crime Insurance Is Hard to Get
Citizen's War on Crime
Worldwide Rise in Street Crime
Has Crime Passed Its Peak?
Crime Wave Hits Colleges
Progress In the Battle Against Crime
Drug Problem—New Moves by the White
    House
A Drive at Heart of the Drug Problem

Crime: 1 in 36 Is a Victim

Newsweek
The President: War on Drugs
America's Battle Against the White Death
The City Killer
The Pushers Pushed
The Heroin Plague: What Can Be Done?

Time
Detroit: Heroin Shooting War
What's Wrong With Drug Education?
The New Public Enemy Number 1

1970

U.S. News
Drug Menace: How Serious?
What's Needed to Speed Up Justice
Crime Costs to Taxpayers Are Soaring
Outlook: A Sharp Decline in Hijackings
Fresh Disclosures on Drugs and GI's
Another Checkup on Drug Use by GI's

War on Drugs: Its Meaning to Tourists
Broader Attack on Drug Abuse
Booming Traffic in Drugs: Goverment's
    Dilemma
Getting Heroin Into U.S.: How Smugglers
    Operate
Marijuana: It's Big Business Now

Moving Forward: Drug Abuse Bill
Nixon's Plea: Stop Making Criminals Heroes
A Leader in Drive to Cut Crime
As Nixon Sees the Future
More Aid for Cities in War Against Crime
Crime-Control Act for Capital—Model for Nation?
Crime Still Rising, but Pace Is Slower
A Terrible Breakdown in Criminal Justice
Why Streets Are Not Safe
Only the People as a Whole Can Cure Crime
Student Violence Widens Range
Citizen's War on Crime: Spreading Across U.S.
How to Stop Rise in Crime
Anticrime Pace in Congress: Much Talk, Little Action

Police Under Attack but Standing Fast
Future Cities: Armed Forts?
War vs. the Police—Officers Tell Their Story
Crime Expense: Now Up to 51 Billion a Year
From Congress: New Anticrime Laws
Booming Industry—Home Safeguards

Newsweek
Narcotics: New Look

Time
The Pursuit of the Poppy
If Pot Were Legal
The Junior Junkie
The Congress: No-Knock Drug Bill
Kids and Heroin: The Adolescent Epidemic
What the Police Can and Cannot Do about Crime
Public Safety and Private Rights

1969

U.S. News
Drug Usage: A Two-Way Attack
Blueprint for a Drug Crackdown
Dope Control
Growing Drive Against Drugs
Growing Menace of Drugs—Nixon's Plan to Fight It
Marijuana: What It Is—and Isn't
Crime War: Key Senator Launches Broad Attack
Fighting Crime in America

If Crime Goes Unchecked: What Big Cities Will Be Like
Crime War: The Nixon Team's Model Plan
One Way to Handle Crime

Newsweek
The Pot Spotters
Pot: Year of the Famine
The Administration: Gangbusters

Time
Drugs: A New Move for Reform
Crime: Blotter for the First Year

1968

U.S. News
Alarming Rise in Dope Traffic
Any Answer to Riots?
   To Shoot or Not To Shoot
Crime Problem: Why It's Not Solved
Disorder in U.S. At A Climax
   Violence Can Only Destroy Us
A Liberal Looks at Violence in U.S.
Runaway Crime: Will Congress Act?
What Courts Are Doing to Law Enforcement
The Story of Crime in U.S.
Tide Turning Against Criminals

Reversing Crime Trend
Crackdown on Criminals—How It Worked in One City
Congress: A Veto Coming?
When a State Opens Its Own War on Crime
Where War Has Been Declared on Hoodlums

Newsweek
How to Win the War
Cities: Crime and Punishment

Time
Crime and Counterforce

1967

U.S. News
Era of Growing Strife in U.S.
What to Do about Crime in U.S.
Is There a Sick Society in the U.S.?
What Happens When Rioters Get into Court
Who Commits the Crimes? Repeaters, Says FBI

War, Riots, Crime . . . Why Dems Worry about '68

Newsweek
The President: A Delicate Balance

Time
Crusading in Indianapolis

1966

U.S. News
When a State Tries to Clean Itself Up
Compassion for Punks
FBI's War on Organized Crime
More Criminals to Go Free: Effect of Court's Ruling
What Has Happened to Moral Climate in America?

Newsweek
No Way Out?

Time
Supreme Court: New Rules for Police Rooms
Criminal Justice: An End to Copping
Crime: Meaningless Statistics?

1965

U.S. News
Crime Runs Wild—Are Courts to Blame? Or Police? Or Society?
Crime Runs Wild—Will It Be Halted?
  We Mollycoddle Criminals
Is Crime in U.S. Out of Hand?
  How Supreme Court Is Curbing Police
  Most of Problem Comes Back to Supreme Court
Speedier Justice in Britain: We Reformed Our Laws in 19th Century and U.S. Didn't
Lawlessness Galore: Why It's Come to the U.S.
Lawlessness in U.S.—Warning From A Top Jurist
Courts Too Soft on Criminals? Warning by AG

As Congress Takes a Hand in War Against Crime
The Criminal Is Living in a Golden Age

Newsweek
Crime: Rising Tide
Crime: Up, Up, Up
Narcotics: Slum to Suburb

Time
Cities: The Malignant Enemy
Criminal Justice: The Confession Controversy
Criminal Justice: Another Confession Problem
Criminal Law: The Court and the Cop
Criminal Justice: Gideon's Impact

1964

U.S. News
Is Crime Running Wild?
How Much Crime Can America Take?
  First Defect Is Among Judges Themselves
  There Is a Tendency to Tolerate Crime

How Criminals Solve Their Investment Problem
An Answer to the Rise in Crime and Violence

Newsweek
Crime and Politics

Time
Criminal Law: Equal Justice for All

1963

U.S. News
Will City Streets Ever Be Safe Again?
Crime Goes on and Gets Worse
Judge Tells How to Deal With Underage Hoods

1962

U.S. News
Who's to Blame for Rising Rate of Crime?
What to Do about Crime in the Big Cities

1961

U.S. News
Where Even Police Are Not Safe
U.S. Crime Wave: Police vs. the Courts
    Judges Forgetting People Have Rights Too

1960

U.S. News
Upsurge in Crime—And Why
    More Crimes, Year By Year
    Many More Laws to Break

1959

U.S. News
Terror Comes to City Streets
    Where Women Are Afraid to Go Out at Night

1958

Newsweek
Crime: Wide Open Town
Crime: Get the 100 Big Ones

1957

U.S. News
Easing Up on Murderers—Why?

Crime: The Seldom Seen

Crime in U.S.—Is It Getting Out of Hand?
Newsweek
Crime: Going Up
Time
Criminal Law: To Balance the Scales

Time
Crime: The Untouchables

Newsweek
Crime: Crackdown
Time
Crime: Is There No Respect?
Inside Dope

Police Efficiency Is Increasing
Time
Even the Unsavory

Another Big Problem for Big Cities
Court Rulings Frustrate Police
Time
Crime: Project Green

Crime: Most Violent Year
Time
Crime: The Rate

Why Policeman's Job Is Getting Tougher

Newsweek
California: Staying the Executioner
Florida: The Old Breed

Legalized Addiction
Crime: $100 Million Crackdown

1956

U.S. News
Crime Is Rising in U.S.
Newsweek
Narcotics: Flood-Tide

Time
Investigations: The Problem of Dope
Drug Detector

1955

U.S. News
First Time in 8 Years: Murders, Robberies
Down
Newsweek
Narcotics: This Enveloping Evil

Time
Dope From Red China
Narcotic Dilemma

References

Abel, C., & Marsh, F. (1984). *Punishment and restitution.* Westport, CT: Greenwood.

Abel, R. (Ed.). (1982). *The politics of informal justice.* New York: Academic Press.

A blueprint to fight crime. (1979, July 23). *U.S. News & World Report,* p. 76.

A drug kingpin goes free. (1988, January 11). *Time,* p. 53.

Allison, M. (1991). Judicious judgments? In L. Samuelson & B. Schissel (Eds.), *Criminal justice: Sentencing issues and reform* (pp. 279-297). Toronto: Garamond.

Alper, B., & Nichols, L. (1981). *Beyond the courtroom.* Lexington, MA: Lexington.

Alston, P. (1981). Peace as human right. *Bulletin of Peace Proposals, 11,* 319-326.

American Bar Association (ABA). (1987). *Dispute resolution program directory.* Washington, DC: Author.

Anderson, D. (1988). *Crimes of justice.* New York: Times Books.

Anderson, G. (1988). Prison violence: Victims behind bars. *America, 159* (16), 430-433.

Anderson, J. R., & Woodard, P. L. (1985). Victim and witness assistance: New state law and the system's response. *Judicature, 68,* 221-224.

Andreas, P. (1990, April 16). Peru's addiction to coca dollars. *The Nation,* pp. 515-518.

A new era of punishment. (1990, May 14). *Newsweek,* pp. 50-51.

Arana, A. (1990, May 13). Cartel's "Rambo" sows death in Colombia. *San Francisco Examiner,* 1, 18.

Are criminals born not made? (1985, October 21). *Time,* p. 94.

Arendt, H. (1958). *The human condition.* New York: Vintage.

Arenson, I., & Ginsburg, C. (1990). Class and cocaine in Colombia. *Lies of Our Times, 1,* 16-17.

Attacking the source. (1989, August 28). *Time,* pp. 10-12.

Austern, D. (1987). *The crime victims book.* New York: Viking.

Back to basics in crime war. (1986, February 17). *U.S. News & World Report,* p. 28.

Balloni, A. (1988). Victimization of drug addicts and human rights. In E. Viano (Ed.), *Crime and its victims* (pp. 267-271). London: Taylor & Francis.

Barak, G. (1986). Feminist connections and movements against domestic violence: Beyond criminal justice reform. *Journal of Crime and Justice, 9,* 139-162.

151

Barak, G. (1988). Newsmaking criminology: Reflections on the media, intellectuals, and crime. *Justice Quarterly, 5,* 56-79.

Barak, G. (1991). *Crimes by the capitalist state.* Albany: State University of New York Press.

Barlett, D. L., & Steele, J. B. (1992). *America: What went wrong?* Kansas City, MO: Andrews & McMeel.

Barlow, D. (1988, June). *Economic crisis and the criminal justice system.* Paper presented at the annual meeting of the American Society of Criminology, Chicago, IL.

Barlow, H. (1976). *Crime victims and the sentencing process.* Paper presented at the Second International Symposium on Victimology, Boston, MA.

Barr, R., & Pease, K. (1990). Crime placement, displacement and deflection. In M. Tonry & N. Morris (Eds.), *Crime and justice: A review of research* (Vol. 12, pp. 29-38). Chicago: University of Chicago Press.

Bass, K. (1992, June). Fighting drugs with empowerment. *Crossroads,* pp. 16-20.

Bassiouni, M. C. (1985). The protection of "collective victims" in international law. *New York Law School Human Rights Annual, 2,* 239-257.

Baum, D. (1992, June 29). The drug war on civil liberties. *The Nation,* pp. 886-888.

Beer, J. (1986). *Peacemaking in your neighborhood.* Philadelphia: New Society.

Behind the violence: Lives without meaning. (1978, December 11). *U.S. News & World Report,* p. 25.

Behind violence: Failure of democracy to get tough. (1981, May 25). *U.S. News & World Report,* p. 25.

Beinen, L. (1981). Rape III: National developments in rape reform legislation. *Women's Law Reporter, 6,* 170-189.

Blair, D. (1990, Summer). Drug war delusions. *SOMA,* pp. 12-14.

Bohm, R. (1986). Crime, criminal and crime-control policy myths. *Justice Quarterly, 3,* 191-214.

Bouza, T. (1989, October 18-24). Pandering to popular fear won't stop crime. *In These Times,* p. 17.

Box-Grainger, J. (1986). Sentencing rapists. In R. Matthews & J. Young (Eds.), *Confronting Crime* (pp. 31-52). London: Sage.

Boyle, F. A. (1988, June). *International law, citizen resistance, and crimes by the state.* Paper presented at the annual meeting of the American Society of Criminology, Chicago, IL.

Brady, J. (1981). Towards popular justice in the U.S. *Contemporary Crises, 5,* 155.

Braithwaite, J. (1979). *Inequality, crime and public policy.* New York: Routledge & Kegan Paul.

Brants, C., & Koh, E. (1986). Penal sanctions as a feminist strategy: Contradiction in terms? *International Journal of the Sociology of Law, 14* (3, 4), 269-286.

Brauer, R. (1990, May 21). The drug war of words. *The Nation,* pp. 705-706.

Bridges, L., & Fekete, L. (1985). Victims, the "urban jungle," and the new racism. *Race and Class, 27,* 45-60.

Brodhead, F., & Herman. E. (1987). *Demonstration elections.* Boston: South End.

Bronstein, A. (1991). U.S. prisons create prison human rights violations. *National Prison Project Journal, 6,* 4-5, 13-14.

Brownstein, H. H. (1991). The media and the construction of random drug violence. *Social Justice, 18* (4), 85-104.

Caringella-MacDonald, S., & Humphries, D. (1991). Sexual assault, women and the community. In H. Pepinsky & R. Quinney (Eds.), *Criminology as peacemaking* (pp. 98-113). Bloomington: Indiana University Press.

Carlisle, J. (1990, Winter). Drug war propaganda. *Propaganda Review,* pp. 14-16.

Carr, C. (1991, April 30). Against her will. *Village Voice,* pp. 36, 38.

Carriere, K., & Ericson, R. (1989). *Crime stoppers: A study in the organization of community policing.* Toronto: University of Toronto Centre of Criminology.

Carrington, F. (1983). *Crime and justice.* Washington, DC: Heritage Foundation.

Carrington, F., & Nicholson, G. (1984). The victims' movement: An idea whose time has come. *Pepperdine Law Review, 11,* 1-14.

Carter, S. (1988). When victims happen to be black. *Yale Law Journal, 97,* 420-447.

Caulfield, S. (1991). The perpetuation of violence through criminological theory. In H. Pepinsky & R. Quinney (Eds.), *Criminology as peacemaking* (pp. 228-238). Bloomington: Indiana University Press.

Cavender, G., & Bond-Maupin, L. (1991). *Fear and loathing on reality television: An analysis of "America's Most Wanted" and "Unsolved Mysteries."* Unpublished paper.

Chambliss, W. J. (1988). Dealing with America's drug problem. In M. Raskin & C. Hartman (Eds.), *Winning America* (pp. 228-235). Boston: South End.

Chambliss, W. J. (1989). State-organized crime. *Criminology, 27,* 183-208.

Chernick, M. W. (1990, April). The drug war. *NACLA Report on the Americas,* pp. 30-39.

Chomsky, N. (1988). *The culture of terrorism.* Boston: South End.

Chomsky, N., & Herman, E. (1979). *The Washington connection and Third World fascism.* Boston: South End.

Christie, N. (1977). Conflicts as property. *British Journal of Criminology, 17* (1), 1-14.

Christie, N. (1982). *The limits to pain.* Oxford, UK: Martin Robertson.

Cipes, R. (1968). *The crime war.* New York: New American Library.

Clark, R. (1992). *War crimes.* Washington, DC: Maisonneuve.

Clarke, F. (1991). Hate violence in the United States. *FBI Law Enforcement Bulletin, 60* (1), 14-17.

Claude, R., & Weston, B. (Eds.). (1989). *Human rights in the international community.* Philadelphia: University of Pennsylvania Press.

Cohen, S. (1985). *Victims of social control.* Oxford, UK: Oxford University Press.

Collett, M. (1988, August 13). The myth of the narco-guerrillas. *The Nation,* pp. 113, 130-134.

Comstock, G. (1981). Social and cultural impact of mass media. In E. Abel (Ed.), *What's news* (pp. 132-150). San Francisco: Institute for Contemporary Studies.

Cook, R., Roehl, J., & Sheppard, D. (1980). *Neighborhood justice centers field test.* Washington, DC: U.S. Department of Justice.

Cooney, R., & Michalowski, H. (1987). *The power of the people.* Philadelphia: New Society.

Cops and cameras: Why TV is slow to cover police brutality. (1991, September-October). *Columbia Journalism Review,* p. 15.

Corn, D. (1988, April 30). Can he lift the C.I.A. veil? Kerry's drug hearings. *The Nation,* pp. 590, 593-594.

Corn, D. (1990, May 14). Justice's war on drug treatment: Throwing away the key. *The Nation,* pp. 659-662.

Corn, D., Gravley, E., & Morley, J. (1989, February 27). Drug czars we've known. *The Nation,* p. 258.

Cotts, C. (1992, March 9). Hard sell in the drug war. *The Nation,* pp. 300-302.

Court rulings frustrate police. (1959, April 6). *U.S. News & World Report,* p. 78.

Courts too easy on crime: Police chiefs speak out. (1972, April 10). *U.S. News & World Report,* p. 52.

Crime: A conspiracy of silence. (1991, May 18). *Newsweek,* p. 37.

Crime stoppers: Citizens get into the act. (1979, September 17). *Time,* p. 84.

Crime victims ask their day in court. (1983, February 7). *U.S. News & World Report,* p. 7.

Culhane, C. (1985). *Still barred from prison.* Montreal: Black Rose.

Cullen, F. T., Maakestad, W. J., & Cavender, G. (1987). *Corporate crime under attack.* Cincinnati: Anderson.

Cullen, F. T., Wozniak, J. F., & Frank, J. (1985). The rise of the elderly offender. *Crime & Social Justice, 23,* 151-165.

Cumberbatch, G., & Beardsworth, A. (1976). Criminals, victims and mass communications. In E. Viano (Ed.), *Victims and society* (pp. 72-90). Washington, DC: Visage.

Currie, E. (1985). *Confronting crime.* New York: Pantheon.

Currie, E. (1989). Confronting crime: looking toward the twenty-first century. *Justice Quarterly, 6* (1), 5-25.

Currie, E. (1991). *Dope and trouble.* New York: Pantheon.

Curry, R. (Ed.). (1988). *Freedom at risk: Secrecy, censorship and repression in the eighties.* Philadelphia: Temple University Press.

Daly, K. (1989, Winter). Criminal justice ideologies and practices in different voices: Some feminist questions about justice. *International Journal of the Sociology of Law,* pp. 57-64.

Danielus, H. (1986). The United Nations fund for torture victims. *Human Rights Quarterly, 8,* 294-305.

Darnell, R. O., Else, J., & Wright, R. D. (Eds.). (1979). *Alternatives to prisons: Issues and options.* Iowa City: University of Iowa School of Social Work.

Davis, M. (1988). Los Angeles: Civil liberties between the hammer and the rock. *New Left Review, 170,* 37-60.

Davis, M. (1992). The Los Angeles inferno. *Socialist Review, 22* (1), 57-80.

Davis, R. C. (1983). Victim/witness noncooperation. *Journal of Criminal Justice, 11,* 287-299.

Davis, R. C., & Dill, F. (1978). *Comparative study of victim participation in criminal court decisionmaking.* Unpublished paper. New York: Vera Institute of Justice.

Davis, R., Tichane, M., & Grayson, D. (1980). *Mediation and arbitration as alternatives to criminal prosecution in felony cases.* New York: Vera Institute of Justice.

DeCataldo Neuberger, L. (1985). An appraisal of victimological perspectives in international law. *Victimology, 10,* 700-709.

de Haan, W. (1990). *The politics of redress.* London: Unwin Hyman.

de Haan, W. (1991). Abolition and crime control. In K. Stenson & D. Cowell (Eds.), *The politics of crime control* (pp. 203-217). London: Sage.

Delacoste, F., & Newman, F. (Eds.). (1981). *Fight back! Feminist resistance to male violence.* Minneapolis, MN: Cleis.

Dermota, K. (1989, August 15). Where the L-word can get you killed. *Village Voice,* pp. 16-17.

Devitt, T., & Downey, J. Downey. (1991, May/June). Battered women take a beating from the media. *Extra!,* pp. 10-12.

Devitt, T., & Rhodes, S. (1991, April 26). Media and rape. *Christian Science Monitor,* p. 10.

Dittenhoffer, T., & Ericson, R. (1992). The victim/offender reconciliation program. In E. A. Fattah (Ed.), *Towards a critical victimology* (pp. 311-346). London: Macmillan.

Domestic surveillance. (1989). *Covert Action Information Bulletin, 31,* 1-97.

Dope from Red China. (1956, March 21). *Time,* p. 18.

Dorsen, N. (1984). *Our endangered rights.* New York: Pantheon.

Doyle, K., & Statman, M. (1988, May 21). A dirty war. *The Nation,* p. 701.

Drug summit. (1990, April). *World Press Review,* p. 54.

Dunbar, L. (Ed.). (1984). *Minority report.* New York: Pantheon.

Dussich, J. P. J. (1976, July). *The victim advocate: A proposal for comprehensive victim services.* Paper presented at the Second International Symposium on Victimology, Boston, MA.

Duster, T. (1970). *The legislation of morality: Law, drugs and moral judgment.* New York: Free Press.

Dworkin, A. (1991, Summer). The third rape. *Media Watch*, pp. 1-2.

Dykes, D. (1983). American blacks as perpetual victims. In J. Scherer & G. Shepard (Eds.), *Victimization of the Weak* (pp. 53-79). Springfield, IL: Charles C Thomas.

Edelman, M. (1988). *Constructing the political spectacle*. Chicago: University of Chicago Press.

Edwards, S. (1989). *Policing domestic violence*. London: Sage.

Ehrenreich, B. (1989, March-April). Drug frenzy: Why the war on drugs misses the real target. *Utne Reader*, pp. 76-81.

Ehrenreich, B. (1990). *The worst times of our lives*. New York: Vintage.

Eide, A. (1986). The human rights movement and the transformation of the international order. *Alternatives, 11*, 367-402.

Eisenstein, J., & Jacob, H. (1977). *Felony justice*. Boston: Little, Brown.

Elias, R. (1982, July-August). Citizen participation in criminal justice: A critique. *Citizen Participation*, pp. 3-5.

Elias, R. (1983). The symbolic politics of victim compensation. *Victimology, 8*, 103-112.

Elias, R. (1984). *Victims of the system*. New Brunswick, NJ: Transaction.

Elias, R. (1985a). Transcending our social reality of victimization: Toward a new victimology of human rights. *Victimology, 10*, 6-25.

Elias, R. (1985b, Summer). Victims and crime prevention: A basis for social change? *Citizen Participation*, pp. 22-28.

Elias, R. (1990). *The politics of victimization: Victims, victimology and human rights*. New York: Oxford University Press.

Elias, R. (1992a). Community control, criminal justice and victim services. In E. A. Fattah (Ed.), *Towards a critical victimology* (pp. 372-400). London: Macmillan.

Elias, R. (1992b). *Crime control as a peace movement*. Paper presented at Peace Studies Association Conference, Boulder, CO.

Elias, R. (1993a). Gulf wars and crime wars: A culture of violent solutions. In J. Turpin & L. Kurtz (Eds.), *The web of violence* (pp. 74-86). Berkeley: University of California Press.

Elias, R. (1993b). *New culture, less crime: A radical human rights strategy*. Bloomington: Indiana University Press.

Elias, R. (1993c). Police as victims of law and order. *Social Justice, 19* (3), 67-76.

Elias, R., & Turpin, J. (Eds.). (1992, Spring). Peace economies. *Peace Review*, pp. 1-48.

Eliasoph, N. (1986). Drive-in mortality, child abuse, and the media. *Socialist Review, 16*, 7-31.

Ellison, K. (1982). On the victims' side: A "bill of rights" or political hype? *National Law Journal, 46*, 1.

Elvin, J. (1991). U.S. now leads world in rate of incarceration. *National Prison Project Journal, 6*, 1-2.

Engelsman, E. (1990, Summer). The Dutch model. *New Perspectives Quarterly*, pp. 44-45.

Epstein, R. J. (1977). *Agency of fear*. New York: G. P. Putnam.

Ericson, R., Baranek, P., & Chan, J. (1991). *Representing order: Crime, law and justice in the news media*. Toronto: University of Toronto Press.

Estrich, S. (1987). *Real rape*. Cambridge, MA: Harvard University Press.

Experiments in boot camp. (1989, May 22). *Newsweek*, pp. 42-44.

Falk, R. (1981). *Human rights and state sovereignty*. New York: Holmes & Meier.

Falk, R. (1987). The global promise of social movements. In S. H. Mendlovitz & R. B. J. Walker (Eds.), *Towards a just world peace: Perspectives from social movements* (pp. 363-386). Boston: Butterworths.

Faludi, S. (1991). *Backlash: The undeclared war against American women*. New York: Crown Books.

Fattah, E. A. (1986). Prologue: On some visible and hidden dangers of victim movements. In E. A. Fattah (Ed.), *From crime policy to victim policy* (pp. 1-14). London: Macmillan.

Fattah, E. A. (1989). Victims of abuse of power. In E. A. Fattah (Ed.), *The plight of crime victims in modern society* (pp. 29-73). New York: St. Martin's.

Fattah, E. A. (Ed.) (1991). *Understanding criminal victimization.* Englewood Cliffs, NJ: Prentice-Hall.

Fattah, E. A. (Ed.) (1992a). The need for a critical victimology. In E. A. Fattah (Ed.), *Towards a critical victimology* (pp. 3-26). London: Macmillan.

Fattah, E. A. (Ed.). (1992b). *Towards a critical victimology.* London: Macmillan.

Fattah, E. A. (1992c). The United Nations declaration of basic principles of justice for victims of crime and abuse of power. In E. A. Fattah (Ed.), *Towards a critical victimology* (pp. 401-424). London: Macmillan.

Fear of crime haunts U.S. (1980, September 29). *Newsweek,* p. 85.

Feeley, M. (1979). *The process Is the punishment.* New York: Russell Sage.

Ferraro, K. (1989). Policing woman battering. *Social Problems, 36* (1), 61-74.

Fighting back. (1989). *Time.*

Fishman, M. (1978). Crime waves as ideology. *Social Problems, 25,* 531-543.

Fishman, M. (1980). *Manufacturing the news.* Austin: University of Texas Press.

Fitzgerald, M. (1990, May 26). Covering crime. *Editor & Publisher,* pp. 14-15.

Flicker, B. (1990). To jail or not to jail? *ABA Journal, 76,* 64-67.

Foraker-Thompson, J. (1988, June). *Crime and ethics in government: Constitutional crisis.* Paper presented at annual meeting of American Society of Criminology, Chicago, IL.

Forer, L. (1980). *Criminals and victims.* New York: Norton.

Forst, G., & Herndon, J. (1985). The criminal justice response to victim harm. *NIJ Research in Brief,* pp. 1-4.

Forsythe, D. (1989). *Human rights and world politics.* Lincoln: University of Nebraska Press.

Frank, N. (1985). *Crimes against health and safety.* New York: Harrow & Heston.

Frappier, J. (1984). Above the law: Violations of international law by the U.S. government. *Crime & Social Justice, 23,* 1-45.

Fraser, L. (1990, March 28). Cruel and unusual journalism. *San Francisco Bay Guardian,* p. 14.

French, M. (1992). *The war on women.* New York: Summit.

Fresh disclosures on drugs and GIs. (1970, July 6). *U.S. News & World Report,* p. 28.

Friedrichs, D. (1983, April). Victimology: A consideration of the radical critique. *Crime & Delinquency,* pp. 283-294.

Future cities: Armed forts? (1970, September 21). *U.S. News & World Report,* p. 39.

Galaway, B. (1977). The uses of restitution. *Crime and Delinquency, 23,* 57-67.

Galaway, B. (1984). Victim participation in the penal-corrective process. *Victimology, 10,* 617-629.

Galtung, J. (1980). *The true worlds.* New York: Free Press.

Garcia Marquez, G. (1990). The future of Colombia. *Granta, 31,* 87-95.

Garner, R. A. (1980). *Social movements in America.* Chicago: Rand McNally.

Garofalo, J. (1981). Crime and the mass media. *Journal of Research in Crime and Delinquency, 18,* 319-349.

Garofalo, J., & Connelly, K. (1980, September). Dispute resolution centers. *Criminal Justice Abstracts,* pp. 416-461.

Geis, G., Chappell, D., & Agopian, M. W. (1985). Toward the alleviation of human suffering. *Rapporteurs' Report.* 5th International Symposium on Victimology, Jerusalem, Israel.

Genetic traits predispose some to criminality. (1985, April 15). *U.S. News & World Report,* p. 44.

George, N. (1990). *Stop the violence: Overcoming self-destruction.* New York: Pantheon.

Getting tough on cocaine. (1988, November 28). *Newsweek* pp. 76-78.

Gibbons, T. (1988, September). Victims again. *American Bar Association Journal*, pp. 23-29.

Giordana, A. (1990, January-February). Who drafted the press? *Washington Journalism Review*, pp. 23-24.

Gitlin, T. (1989, November-December). The war on drugs and the enlisted press. *Columbia Journalism Review*, pp. 17-18.

Gitlin, T. (1992, April 19). Uncivil society. *Image*, pp. 13-17.

Glasser, I. (1991, August). Talking liberties: Let's get real on crime. *Civil Liberties*, p. 3.

Glasser, I., & Siegel, L. (1991). *When constitutional rights seem too extravagent to endure.* Unpublished paper.

Goldstein, R. (1988, September 30). Drugs are us: Getting real about getting high. *Village Voice*, pp. 21-24.

Goldstein, R. J. (1978). *Political repression in modern America.* Cambridge, MA: Schenkman.

Gordon, D. (1990). *The justice juggernaut.* New Brunswick, NJ: Rutgers University Press.

Gordon, M., & Heath, L. (1981). The news business, crime and fear. In D. Lewis (Ed.), *Reactions to crime* (pp. 57-69). Beverly Hills, CA: Sage.

Gordon, R. M. (1986). Financial abuse of the elderly and state "protective services." *Crime & Social Justice, 26,* 116-134.

Gorriti, G. (1990, Summer). Southern exposure: The view from Peru. *New Perspectives Quarterly*, pp. 49-51.

Gould, S. J. (1990, April). The war on (some) drugs. *Harper's*, pp. 24-26.

Graber, D. (1980). *Crime news and the public.* New York: Praeger.

Grassi, J. (1991). Is gun control legislation a solution for protecting victims? In D. Sank & D. Caplin (Eds.), *To be a victim* (pp. 103-110). New York: Plenum.

Great Atlantic Radio. (1990). *War on drugs.* Baltimore: Author.

Green, M., & Berry, J. (1985). *The challenge of hidden profits: White-collar crime as big business.* New York: William Morrow.

Greenwood, P. (1982). *Preventive incapacitation.* Santa Monica, CA: Rand Corporation.

Greider, W. (1992). *Who will tell the people: The betrayal of American democracy.* New York: Simon & Schuster.

Grietz, J. (1990). *A nation betrayed.* New York: Lazarus.

Gross, B. (1980). *Friendly fascism.* New York: M. Evans.

Groves, W. B., & Newman, G. (1986). *Punishment and privilege.* New York: Harrow & Heston.

"Growing menace" of drugs—Nixon's plan to fight it. (1971, July 28). *U.S. News & World Report,* p. 60.

Grube, J. (1990, February-March). Drugs, financial aid, and you. *Off the Record, 7* (3), p. 1.

Gusfield, J. (1981). *The culture of public problems.* Chicago: University of Chicago Press.

Hackett, G. (1989, May 29). On the firing line. *Newsweek,* pp. 32-36.

Hall, D. J. (1975). The role of the victim in the prosecution and disposition of a criminal case. *Vanderbilt Law Review, 28,* 932-975.

Halleck, S. (1980). Vengeance and victimization. *Victimology, 5,* 99-109.

Hamill, P. (1991, July). A confederacy of complainers. *Esquire*, pp. 26-30.

Haminer, W. (1992). *I'm dysfunctional, you're dysfunctional.* Reading, MA: Addison-Wesley.

Hamowy, R. (1987). *Dealing with drugs: The consequences of government control.* Lexington, MA: D.C. Heath.

Hanmer, J., Radford, J., & Stanko, E. (1989). *Women, policing and male violence.* New York: Routledge.

Harland, A. (1982). Monetary remedies for the victims of crime: Assessing the role of the criminal courts. *UCLA Law Review, 30,* 52-128.

Harland, A. (1983). One hundred years of restitution. *Victimology, 8,* 190-202.

Harland, A., & Harris, P. W. (1984). Developing and implementing alternatives to incarceration: A problem of planned change in criminal justice. *University of Illinois Law Review,* pp. 319-364.

Harrington, C. (1985). *Shadow justice.* Westport, CT: Greenwood.

Harris, C. (1990, June 27). San Francisco narcotics cops make big bucks off the war on drugs. *San Francisco Bay Guardian,* pp. 8-9.

Harris, M. K. (1991). Moving into the new millennium: Toward a feminist vision of justice. In H. Pepinsky & R. Quinney (Eds.), *Criminology as peacemaking* (pp. 83-97). Bloomington: Indiana University Press.

Harvey, M. (1988, May-June). Why the left is wrong about crime. *Utne Reader,* pp. 10-11.

Has Mexico matched up on drugs? DEA agents say no. *Newsweek* (1985).

Hayeslip, D. W. (1989, March-April). Local-level drug enforcement: New strategies. *NIJ Reports,* pp. 2-7.

Henderson, J., & Gitchoff, G. T. (1980, April). *Victim perceptions of alternatives to incarceration: An exploratory study.* Paper presented at the First World Congress of Victimology, Washington, DC.

Henderson, L. N. (1985). The wrongs of victim's rights. *Stanford Law Review, 37,* 937-1021.

Henry, W. (1986, October 6). Reporting the drug problem. *Time,* p. 73.

Henson, M. (1991). No more rules of thumb. *Glamour, 89,* 108-110.

Hentig, J. (1984). *Citizens against crime: An assessment of the Neighborhood Watch Program in Washington, D.C.* Occasional Papers. Washington, DC: George Washington University Center for Washington Area Studies.

Hentoff, N. (1986, September). Presumption of guilt. *The Progressive,* p. 10.

Herman, E. (1982). *The real terror network.* Boston: South End.

Herman, E. (1989, November). The "war" on drugs? *Zeta,* pp. 19-20.

Hertzberg, S. (1981). *The protection of human rights in the criminal process under international instruments and national constitutions.* Amsterdam: Eres.

Hills, S. (1987). *Corporate violence.* Savage, MD: Rowman & Littlefield.

Hinckle, W. (1990, May 17-June 28). George Bush and the drug wars. *San Francisco Examiner,* 7-part series.

Hochstedler, E. (Ed.). (1984). *Corporations as criminals.* Beverly Hills, CA: Sage.

Hoffman, A. (1987). *Steal this urine test: Fighting drug hysteria in America.* New York: Penguin.

Hoffman, J. (1990, April 3). Pregnant addicts turned away. *Village Voice,* pp. 11-12.

Hoffman, M. (1983). Victim impact statement. *Western State University Law Review, 10,* 221-245.

Holbrook, C. (1988, March). Victim. *Guideposts,* pp. 2-7.

Hopkins, E. (1989, April 20). Nowhere to run. *Rolling Stone,* pp. 72-78.

Horney, J., & Spohn, C. (1991). Rape law reform and instrumental change in six urban jurisdictions. *Law and Society Review, 25,* 117-153.

How Supreme Court is curbing police. (1965, October 4). *U.S. News & World Report,* p. 53.

How to win the war. (1968, July 3). *Newsweek,* p. 32.

Hubbell, M. M. (1987). Who pays for the cure? Restitution for adolescent rape victims. *Journal of Contemporary Law, 13,* 301-330.

Humphries, D. (1981). Serious crime, news coverage, and ideology. *Crime and Delinquency, 27,* 191-205.

Hutchings, N. (1988). *The violent family.* New York: Human Sciences.

Hutchinson, E. O. (1989, May/June). So sayeth *Newsweek* on crime. *Extra!,* p. 5.

Hutchinson, E. O. (1990a). *Crime, drugs and African-Americans.* Unpublished paper.

Hutchinson, E. O. (1990b). *The mugging of black America.* Chicago: African American Images.

Hutchinson, E. O. (1991, June). Politics, the media, and the LAPD. *Lies of Our Times,* pp. 4-5.

Immarigeon, R. (1991). Beyond the fear of crime. In H. Pepinsky & R. Quinney (Eds.), *Criminology as peacemaking* (pp. 69-80). Bloomington: Indiana University Press.

Irwin, J. (1981). *Prisons in turmoil.* Glenview, IL: Scott, Foresman.

Is nature to blame for careers of crime? (1986, February 10). *U.S. News & World Report,* p. 67.

Is there a sick society in the U.S.? (1967, February 20). *U.S. News & World Report,* p. 48.

Is TV news hyping America's cocaine problem? (1990, April 26). *TV Guide,* pp. 4-6.

It doesn't have to be like this. (1989, September 2). *The Economist,* pp. 21-24.

Ivans, M. (1990, February). The czar is hooked. *The Progressive,* p. 38.

James, J. (1992, February). Media convictions, fair-trial activism, and the Central Park case. *Z Magazine,* pp. 33-37.

Jankowski, M. S. (1992). *Islands in the streets: Gangs and American urban society.* Berkeley: University of California Press.

Jobson, K. (1983). The parole board: What liability to victims? *Dalhousie Law Journal, 7,* 528-547.

Johnson, R., & Bielski, V. (1990, May 9). Recovering for two. *San Francisco Bay Guardian,* pp. 23-24.

Johnson, T. V. (1990, May 3). War on drugs is cover for attack on black community. *This World,* p. 6.

Johnston, S. (1974). Toward a supra-national criminology: The right and duty of victims of national government to seek defense through world law. In I. Drapkin & E. Viano (Eds.), *Victimology: Theoretical issues* (pp. 37-44). Lexington, MA: Lexington.

Johnston, S. (1978). Instituting criminal justice in the global village. In E. Viano (Ed.), *Victims and society* (pp. 325-332). Washington, DC: Visage.

Jones, T. (1988). *Corporate killing.* London: Free Association.

Jordan, J. (1992, May 6). Burning all illusions tonight. *S.F. Bay Guardian,* pp. 15, 18, 20.

Kahn, L. A. (1982). Constitutionality of the Victim & Witness Protection Act of 1982. *Federal Probation, 48,* 81-82.

Kaplan, D. (1991, December 16). Remove that blue dot. *Newsweek,* p. 26.

Karmen, A. (1984). *Crime victims.* Belmont, CA: Brooks/Cole.

Karp, W. (1988, November). Liberty under siege. *Harper's,* pp. 53-67.

Kasarda, J. D. (1990, Summer). Opportunity foreclosure zones. *New Perspectives Quarterly,* pp. 16-21.

Katz, J. (1980). The social movement against white-collar crime. In E. Bitner & S. Messinger (Eds.), *Criminology review yearbook* (Vol. 2, pp. 162-183). Beverly Hills, CA: Sage.

Katz, L. (1990, February 12). TV's war on reality. *San Francisco Weekly,* p. 41.

Kavell, J. A. (1989, October). Sending in army could drag U.S. into morass. *In These Times,* p. 11, 22.

Kawell, J. A. (1990, April). Drug wars: The rules of the game. *NACLA Report on the Americas,* pp. 9-10.

Kelly, D. (1990). Victim participation in the criminal justice system. In A. Lurigio, W. Skogan, & R. Davis (Eds.), *Victims of crime* (pp. 172-187). Newbury Park, CA: Sage.

Kelly, D. P. (1987, Summer). How can we help the victim without hurting the defendant? *Criminal Justice, 2,* 14-17.

Kelly, L., & Radford, J. (1987). The problem of men: Feminist perspectives on sexual violence. In P. Scraton (Ed.), *Law, order and the authoritarian state* (pp. 237-253). Philadelphia: Open University Press.

Kelman, H., & Hamilton, V. L. (1989). *Crimes of obedience.* New Haven, CT: Yale University Press.

Kim, S. (1983). *The quest for a just world order.* Boulder, CO: Westview.

Kimmich, M. H. (1985). *America's children: Who cares? Growing needs and declining assistance in the Reagan era.* Washington, DC: Urban Institute Press.

King, R. (1989, October 23). A worthless crusade. *Newsweek,* pp. 7-8.

Kinoy, A. (1988). The present constitutional crisis. In J. Lobel (Ed.), *A less than perfect union* (pp. 32-40). New York: Monthly Review Press.

Kinsey, R., Lea, J., & Young, J. (1986). *Losing the fight against crime.* New York: Basil Blackwell.

Kirk, R. (1989, Summer). Behind the cocaine curtain. *Extra!,* pp. 12-13.

Klare, M. T. (1990, January 1). Fighting drugs with the military. *The Nation,* pp. 8-12.

Klare, M. T., & Arnson, C. (1981). *Supplying repression.* Washington, DC: Institute for Policy Studies.

Klein, A. (1988). *Alternative sentencing.* Cincinnati, OH: Anderson.

Klein, L., Luxenburg, J., & Gunther, J. (1991). Taking a bite out of social injustice. In H. Pepinsky & R. Quinney (Eds.), *Criminology as peacemaking* (pp. 280-286). Bloomington: Indiana University Press.

Knoll, E. (1989, October). The phony war on drugs. *The Progressive,* pp. 8-9.

Knoll, E. (1990, June 9). Drug war's real targets. *The Progressive,* p. 9.

Knopp, F. H. (1976). *Instead of prisons: A handbook for abolitionists.* Orwell, VT: Safer Society Press.

Knopp, F. H. (1991). Community solutions to sexual violence: Feminist/abolitionist perspectives. In H. Pepinsky & R. Quinney (Eds.), *Criminology as peacemaking* (pp. 181-193). Bloomington: Indiana University Press.

Kopkind, A. (1990, February 5). Race, class and murder in Boston. *The Nation,* pp. 150, 153-154.

Krasno, M. R. (1983). The Victim & Witness Protection Act of 1982: Does it promise more than the system can deliver? *Judicature, 66,* 469-471.

Kruger, H. (1980). *The great heroin coup.* Boston: South End.

Kwitny, J. (1987). *The crimes of patriots.* New York: Simon & Schuster.

LaCroix, S. (1989, May 1). Jailing mothers for drug abuse. *The Nation,* pp. 585-88.

Lamborn, L. (1987a). The United Nations declaration on victims: Incorporating "abuse of power." *Rutgers Law Journal, 19,* 59-95.

Lamborn, L. (1987b). Victim participation in the criminal justice process: Proposals for a constitutional amendment. *Wayne Law Review, 34,* 125-220.

Lapham, L. (1989, December). A political opiate. *Harper's,* p. 45.

Lappe, F. M., Collins, J., & Kinley, D. (1980). *Aid as obstacle.* San Francisco: Institute for Food and Development Policy.

Lawson, B. (1991). African Americans, criminal victimization and political obligations. In D. Sank & D. Caplin (Eds.), *To be a victim* (pp. 141-158). New York: Plenum.

Lazere, D. (1990a, May 8). Crack and AIDS: The next wave? *Village Voice,* pp. 29-30.

Lazere, D. (1990b, January 23). The drug war is killing us. *Village Voice,* pp. 22-29.

Ledbetter, J. (1991, April 30). O times, O mores: All the innuendos fit to print. *Village Voice,* pp. 36-38.

Lee, R. (1978). Credibility of newspaper and TV news. *Journalism Quarterly, 55,* 282-287.

Lernoux, P. (1988, March 5). Colombia can't kick drugs alone. *The Nation,* pp. 289, 306-308.

Levine, H. G., & Reinarman, C. (1987, March 28). Abusing drug abuse. *The Nation,* pp. 388-390.

Levine, M. (1990). *Deep cover.* New York: Delacorte.

Lewin, T. (1992, May 10). Feminists wonder if it was progress to become "victims." *New York Times*, p. E1.

Lichter, L., & Lichter, S. R. (1983). *Prime time crime*. Washington, DC: Media Institute.

Lightner, C. (1984, Spring). M.A.D.D. at the court. *Judge's Journal*, pp. 36-39.

Living with crime USA. (1972, December 18). *Newsweek*, pp. 31-34.

Lobel, J. (Ed.). (1988). *A less than perfect union*. New York: Monthly Review Press.

Lopez-Rey, M. (1985). *A guide to United Nations criminal policy*. New York: United Nations.

Lotz, R. (1988, June). *Crime in the news*. Paper presented at meeting of the American Society of Criminology, Chicago, IL.

Lurigio, A. J., Skogan, W., & Davis, R. (Eds.). (1990). *Victims of Crime*. Newbury Park, CA: Sage.

Lusane, C. (1991). *Pipe dream blues*. Boston: South End.

Lusane, C., & Desmond, D. (1989, October 11). U.S. pushes drug business on Third World. *The Guardian*, p. 7.

Lynch, M., & Groves, W. B. (1989). *A primer in radical criminology*. New York: Harrow & Heston.

Lynch, M., McDowall, D., & Newman, G. R. (1988, June). *Crime in the world system*. Paper presented at the annual meeting of the American Society of Criminology. Chicago, IL.

Mabry, M., & Thomas, E. (1992), May 18). Crime: A conspiracy of silence. *Newsweek*, p. 37.

MacLennan, C. (1992, January 26). Rehabilitation causes optimism. *The Press* [New Zealand], p. 23.

MacManus, S. A., & Van Hightower, N. R. (1989). Limits of state constitutional guarantees: Lessons from efforts to implement domestic violence policies. *Public Administration Review, 49* (3), 269-277.

Magagnini, F. (1983, May 16). Drunk case judges mad at monitors. *San Francisco Chronicle*, p. 1.

Maguire, M., & Pointing, J. (Eds.). (1988). *Victims of crime*. Philadelphia: Open University.

Maher, L. (1990). Criminalizing pregnancy. *Critical Criminologist, 2*, 1-2, 8.

Making sense of alarms. (1986, August 4). *U.S. News & World Report*, pp. 49-50.

Mama, A. (1989). *The hidden struggle*. London: Race and Housing Research Group.

Marable, M, (1983). *How capitalism underdeveloped black America*. Boston: South End.

Marable, M. (1989, March 8). Community organizing combats crime. *The Guardian*, p. 2.

Margaronis, M. (1990, January 30). Fright knight. *Village Voice*, p. 45.

Martino, M. (1991). Seven alternative punishment programs that work. *National Prison Project Journal, 6*, 2-4.

Martz, L. (1990, February 19). A dirty drug secret. *Newsweek*, pp. 74-77.

Marullo, S., & Hlavacek, J. (1992, Fall). Sociologists on war as a social problem. *Peace Review*, pp. 9-11.

Marx, G. T. (1983). Social control and victimization. *Victimology, 8*, 54-79.

Marx, G. T. (1988). *Under cover: Police surveillance in America*. Berkeley: University of California Press.

Massing, M. (1990, February 5). Drugbusters! *The Nation*, pp. 152-153.

Matthews, R., & Young, J. (1986). *Confronting crime*. London: Sage.

Mauer, M. (1991). *Americans behind bars*. Washington, DC: Sentencing Project.

McConahay, M. J., & Kirk, R. (1989, February/March). Over there: America's drug war abroad. *Mother Jones*, pp. 37-42.

McCoy, A. (1984). *The politics of heroin in Southeast Asia*. New Haven, CT: Yale University Press.

McDonald, W. (1976, July). *Notes on the victim's role in the prosecutorial and dispositional stages of the American criminal justice process.* Paper presented at the Second International Symposium on Victimology, Boston, MA.

McDonald, W. (1979). The prosecutor's domain. In W. McDonald (Ed.), *The prosecutor* (pp. 15-52). Beverly Hills, CA: Sage.

McGillis, D. (1986). *NIJ Issues and practices: Crime victim restitution.* Washington, DC: U.S. Department of Justice.

McGrath, M. (1990, March 16). Anatomy of an epidemic. *East Bay Express,* p. 3.

McLeod, M. (1986). Victim participation at sentencing. *Criminal Law Bulletin, 22,* 501-509.

McLeod, M. (1987). An examination of the victim's role at sentencing: Results of a survey of probation administrators. *Judicature, 71,* 162-172.

McPherson, L. (1992, April/May). News media, racism and the drug war. *Extra!,* p. 5.

McShane, M., & Williams, F. (1992). Radical victimology: A critique of the concept of victim in traditional victimology. *Crime and Delinquency, 38* (2), 258-271.

Meier, R., & Geis, G. (1978). The abuse of power as a criminal activity. In G. Geis (Ed.), *On white collar crime* (pp. 173-184). Beverly Hills, CA: Sage.

Melup, I. (1991). United Nations: Victims of crime. *International Review of Victimology, 2* (1), 29-59.

Messerschmidt, J. (1986). *Capitalism, patriarchy and crime.* Totowa, NJ: Rowman & Allenheld.

Meyer, P. (1981). Communities as victims of corporate crimes. In B. Galaway & J. Hudson (Eds.), *Perspectives on crime victims* (pp. 33-43). St. Louis: C. V. Mosby.

Michalowski, R. J. (1985). *Order, law and crime.* New York: Random House.

Miedzian, M. (1991). *Boys will be boys.* New York: Doubleday.

Miller, M. (1990, January 29). A failed "test case": Washington's drug war. *Newsweek,* pp. 28-29.

Mishra, V. M. (1979). How commercial television networks cover news of law enforcement. *Journalism Quarterly, 56,* 611-617.

Mokiber, R. (1988). *Corporate crime and violence.* San Francisco: Sierra Books.

Monteiro, T. (1990, March 13). Criminalizing African-Americans. *Daily World,* p. 9.

Moore, E., & Mills, M. (1990). The neglected victims and unexamined costs of white-collar crime. *Crime and Delinquency, 36* (3), 408-418.

Moore, M. H., & Kleiman, M. A. R. (1989, September). The police and drugs. *NIJ Perspectives on Policing,* pp. 1-13.

Morales, E. (1989). *Cocaine: White gold rush in Peru.* Tucson: University of Arizona Press.

Morgan, J. (1992, March 3). A black woman's guide to the Tyson trial. *Village Voice,* pp. 37-40.

Morgan, J., & Zedner, L. (1992). *Child victims: Crime, impact and criminal justice.* New York: Oxford University Press.

Morgan, P. (1981). From battered wife to program client: The state's shaping of social problems. *Kapitalistate, 9,* 7-41.

Morganthau, T. (1989, September 11). Children of the underclass. *Newsweek,* pp. 16-28.

Morganthau, T. (1990, April 23). Uncivil liberties? *Newsweek,* pp. 18-20.

Morley, J. (1988, August 27). Bush's drug problem—and ours. *The Nation,* pp. 149, 165-169.

Morley, J. (1990, February 19). Crack in the Washington culture. *The Nation,* pp. 221, 236-240.

Murder in the safest places. (1989, June 23). *U.S. News & World Report,* pp. 6-7.

Murray, M. H. (1987). The torture victim protection act. *Columbia Journal of Transnational Law, 25,* 673-715.

Musto, D. F. (1973). *The American disease: The origins of narcotics control.* New Haven, CT: Yale University Press.

Muwakkil, S. (1989, September 27). Drugs and the black community. *In These Times,* p. 15.

Muwakkil, S. (1990, March 14-20). Get-tough crime policies squeeze a generation. *In These Times*, p. 6.

Nadelman, E. (1988, Spring). U.S. drug policy: A bad export. *Foreign Policy*, pp. 83-109.

Nadelman, E. (1992, Spring). America's drug problem: The case for decriminalization. *Dissent*, pp. 205-212.

Nader, R. (1986). The corporate drive to restrict their victims' rights. *Gonzaga Law Review, 22*, 15-28.

Nader, R. (1992). *The Concord principles.* Unpublished mimeo.

National Organization for Victim Assistance (NOVA). (1988). *Victim rights and services: A legislative directory.* Washington, DC: Author.

Naureckas, J. (1991a, July/August). Media activism challenges rape coverage. *Extra!*, p. 19.

Naureckas, J. (1991b, May/June). What is a crisis? *Extra!*, p. 10.

Naureckas, J. (1991c, May/June). Who's the victim? *Extra!*, p. 11.

Naureckas, J., & Ryan, R. (1987, April 15). The lessons of Laos. *In These Times*, pp. 12-13.

Navasky, V. (1990, January 8). Body invaders. *The Nation*, pp. 39-40.

Neier, A. (1982). *Only judgment.* Middletown, CT: Wesleyan University Press.

Newton, A. (1976). Alternatives to imprisonment: Day fines, community service orders, and restitution. *Crime & Delinquency Literature, 8*, 109-120.

Normandeau, A. (1983). For a Canadian and international charter of rights for crime victims. *Canadian Journal of Criminology, 25*, 463-469.

Office for Victims of Crime. (1988). *Report to Congress.* Washington, DC: Government Printing Office.

O'Neill, T. P. (1984). The good, the bad, and the Burger Court: Victim's rights and a new model of criminal review. *Journal of Criminal Law & Criminology, 75*, 363-387.

Only the people as a whole can cure crime. (1970, March 9). *U.S. News & World Report*, p. 92.

O'Sullivan, E. (1978). What has happened to rape crisis centers? *Victimology, 3*, 45-62.

Other Americas Radio. (1990a). *Lines of deceit: Cocaine and the White House.* Santa Barbara, CA: Author.

Other Americas Radio. (1990b). *A nation betrayed: Heroin and the White House.* Santa Barbara, CA: Author.

Pandiani, J. (1978). Crime time TV: If all we knew is what we saw. *Contemporary Crises, 2*, 437-458.

Parato, S. K. (1990). *Make sense, not "war."* Unpublished paper.

Parenti, M. (1986). *Inventing reality.* New York: St. Martin's.

Parenti, M. (1988). *Democracy for the few.* New York: St. Martin's.

Parenti, M. (1991). *Make-believe media.* New York: St. Martin's.

Parker, K. (1991). Criminal victimization among black Americans. *Journal of Black Studies, 22* (2), 186-195.

Pearce, J. (1990, April). Colombia cracks up. *NACLA Report on the Americas*, pp. 12-29.

Pell, E. (1984). *The big chill.* Boston: Beacon.

Pepinsky, H. (1991a). *The geometry of violence and democracy.* Bloomington: Indiana University Press.

Pepinsky, H. (1991b). Peacemaking in criminology and criminal justice. In H. Pepinsky & R. Quinney (Eds.), *Criminology as peacemaking* (pp. 299-327). Bloomington: Indiana University Press.

Pepinsky, H., & Jeslow, P. (1984). *Myths that cause crime.* Cabin John, MD: Seven Locks Press.

Pepinsky, H., & Quinney, R. (Eds.). (1989). *Criminology as peacemaking.* Bloomington: Indiana University Press.

Perspectives on proposals for a constitutional amendment providing victim participation in the criminal justice system [Symposium]. (1987). *Wayne Law Review, 34*, 1-220.

Petit, C. (1988, February 28). A history of habits. *This World*, pp. 7-24.

Phipps, A. (1986). Radical criminology and criminal victimization. In R. Matthews & J. Young (Eds.), *Confronting crime* (pp. 97-117). London: Sage.

Piven, F. F., & Cloward, R. A. (1971). *Regulating the poor.* New York: Vintage.

Piven, F. F., & Cloward, R. A. (1979). *Poor people's movements.* New York: Vintage.

Police under attack but standing fast. (1970, September 21). *U.S. News & World Report*, p. 38.

Pollitt, K. (1991a, June 24). Media goes wilding in Palm Beach. *The Nation*, pp. 47-52.

Pollitt, K. (1991b; November 4). Women scorned. *The Nation*, pp. 540-541.

Posner, A. K. (1984). Victim impact statements and restitution: Making the punishment fit the crime. *Brooklyn Law Review, 50*, 301-338.

President's Task Force on Victims of Crime. (1982). *Final report.* Washington, DC: Government Printing Office.

Price, B., & Sokoloff, N. (1982). Women and victims of crime. In B. Price & N. Sokoloff (Eds.), *The criminal justice system and women* (pp. 185-370). New York: Clark Boardman.

Public safety and private rights. (1970, July 27). *Time*, p. 30.

Quinney, R., & Wildeman, J. (1991). *The problem of crime: a peace & social justice perspective.* Mountain View, CA: Mayfield.

Rabine, M. (1989, March). The war on drugs. *Zeta*, pp. 92-94.

Rabine, M. (Ed.). (1991). The war on drugs. *Social Justice, 18* (4), 1-173.

Radford, J., & Stanko, E. (1991). Violence against women and children: The contradictions of crime control under patriarchy. In K. Stenson & D. Cowell (Eds.), *The politics of crime control* (pp. 186-202). London: Sage.

Rafter, N. H. (1987). Why the left is wrong about crime. *Socialist Review, 17*, 17-34.

Randall, D., Lee-Sammons, L., & Hagner, P. (1988). Crime versus elite crime coverage in network news. *Social Science Quarterly, 69*, 910-929.

Ranish, D., & Shichor, D. (1992). The victim's role in the penal process. In E. A. Fattah (Ed.), *Towards a critical victimology* (pp. 222-237). London: Macmillan.

Rapping, E. (1991, August). The uses of violence. *The Progressive*, p. 36.

Ratner, M. (1987, Summer). Contragate, covert action and the constitution. *Social Policy*, pp. 43-47.

Reasons, C. (1982). Crime and the abuse of power. In P. Wickman & T. Dailey (Eds.), *White collar and economic crime* (pp. 43-55). Lexington, MA: Lexington.

Reconsidering suspects' rights. (1976, May 31). *Time*, p. 75.

Reed, I. (1989, November 20). The black pathology biz: Crime, drugs and the media. *The Nation*, pp. 597-598.

Reed, I. (1992, May 3). Every black person risks becoming a Rodney King. *San Francisco Examiner*, p. A-15.

Regush, N. M. (1971). *The drug addiction business.* New York: Dial.

Reidinger, P. (1989). Trends in the law: unequal protection. *American Bar Association Journal, 75*, 102-103.

Reiman, J. (1984). *The rich get richer and the poor get prison.* New York: John Wiley.

Reinarman, C. (1988). The social construction of a drug problem. *Theory and Society, 17*, 91-120.

Richards, D. A. J. (1982). Drug use and the rights of the person. *Rutgers Law Review, 3*, 178-202.

Ridgeway, J. (1989, September 12). The straight dope. *Village Voice*, pp. 26-27.

Rios, L., & Yeochum, M. (1983, December 18). Making sure drunk drivers pay. *San Jose Mercury News*, p. 1A.

Roshier, B. (1981). The selection of crime news by the press. In S. Cohen & J. Young (Eds.), *The manufacture of news* (pp. 87-99). Beverly Hills, CA: Sage.

ROTC for the nation's cops? (1983, October 3). *Newsweek*, p. 58.

Rubel, H. (1992). Victim participation in sentencing proceedings. In E. A. Fattah (Ed.), *Towards a critical victimology* (pp. 238-259). London: Macmillan.

Rubin, G. (1984). Thinking sex. In C. S. Vance (Ed.), *Pleasure and danger* (pp. 267-319). Boston: Routledge & Kegan Paul.

Rubin, L. (1986). *Quiet rage: Bernard Goetz in a time of madness*. New York: Farrar, Straus & Giroux.

Rudovsky, D. (1988). Crime, law enforcement, and constitutional rights. In J. Lobel (Ed.), *A less than perfect union* (pp. 361-376). New York: Monthly Review Press.

Russell, D. E. H., & Van Den Ven, N. (1984). *Crimes against women*. East Palo Alto, CA: Frog In the Well Press.

Ryan, T. (1985). *Screw*. Boston: South End.

Sacco, V. (1982). The effects of mass media on perceptions of crime. *Pacific Sociological Review, 25*, 475-493.

Sank, D., & Caplin, D. (Eds.). (1991). *To be a victim*. New York: Plenum.

Savan, L. (1989, November 14). Ad-dictions and the drug war. *Village Voice*, pp. 54-56.

Schaaf, R. W. (1986). New international instruments in crime prevention and criminal justice. *International Journal of Legal Information, 14*, 176-182.

Schattenberg, G. (1981). Social control functions of mass media depictions of crime. *Sociological Inquiry, 51*, 71-77.

Scheingold, S. (1974). *The politics of rights*. New Haven, CT: Yale University Press.

Scherer, J., & Shepard, G. (Eds.). (1983). *Victimization of the weak*. Springfield, IL: Charles C Thomas.

Schmoke, K. (1989, Summer). A war for the Surgeon General, not the Attorney General. *New Perspectives Quarterly*, pp. 12-15.

Schneider, A. (1990). *Deterrence and juvenile crime*. New York: Springer-Verlag.

Schuyler, N. (1990). The why of the needle. *San Francisco Weekly, 9*(5), 1, 6.

Scraton, P. (Ed.). (1987). *Law, order and the authortarian state*. Philadelphia: Open University Press.

Scull, A. (1983). *Decarceration*. Englewood Cliffs, NJ: Prentice-Hall.

Scutt, J. A. (1982). Victims, offenders and restitution: Real alternative or panacea? *Australian Law Journal, 56*, 156-167.

Sebba, L. (1982). The victim's role in the penal process: A theoretical orientation. *Australian Journal of Comparative Law, 30*, 217-230.

Sebold, A. (1989, February 26). Speaking of the unspeakable. *New York Times Magazine*, pp. 16-18.

Sedgwick, J. (1992, May). The face of crime in America. *Self*, pp. 128-132, 174.

Seeing justice never done. (1986, February 17). *Time*, p. 73.

Shannon, E. (1988). *Desperados: Latin drug lords, U.S. lawmen, and the war America can't win*. New York: Viking.

Shapiro, C., & Gutierrez, L. (1982, Summer). Crime victims services. *Social Policy*, pp. 50-53.

Sharman, J. R. (1988). Constitutional law: Victim impact statements and the 8th amendment. *Harvard Journal of Law & Public Policy, 11*, 583-593.

Sheptycki, J. W. E. (1991). Using the state to change society: The example of "domestic violence." *Journal of Human Justice, 3* (1), 47-66.

Sherizen, S. (1978). Social creation of crime news: All the news fitted to print. In C. Winick (Ed.), *Deviance and mass media* (pp. 98-111). Beverly Hills, CA: Sage.

Siegel, L. (Ed.). (1989). *Confronting crime: New directions.* New York: American Civil Liberties Union.

Silberman, C. (1978). *Criminal violence, criminal justice.* New York: Vintage.

Skogan, W. (1990). *Disorder and decline.* New York: Free Press.

Slater, P. (1991). *A dream deferred.* Boston: Beacon.

Smart, C. (1989). *Feminism and the power of the law.* London: Routledge.

Smith, B. L. (1985). Trends in the victims' rights movement and implications for future research. *Victimology, 10,* 34-43.

Smith, E. (1992, Summer). The color of news. *Muckraker,* p. 3.

Smith, S. (1986). *Fear or freedom.* Racine, WI: Mother Courage Press.

Smith, S. R., & Freinkel, S. (1988). *Adjusting the balance: Federal policy and victim services.* Westport, CT: Greenwood.

Snider, L. (1988, June). *The potential of the criminal justice system to promote feminist concerns.* Paper presented at annual meeting of the American Society of Criminology, Chicago, IL.

Solomon, A. (1991, August 6). Unreasonable doubt. *Village Voice,* pp. 25-26.

Solomon, N., & Lee, M. (1991). *Unreliable sources.* New York: Lyle Stuart.

Sommer, R. (1976). *The end of imprisonment.* New York: Oxford University Press.

Spence, G. (1988). *Justice for none.* New York: Times Books.

Stark, J., & Goldstein, H. (1985). *The rights of crime victims.* Carbondale, IL: Southern Illinois University Press.

Steele, S. (1992, July). The new sovereignty. *Harper's,* pp. 47-54.

Stein, J. (1988). VOCA revisited, reauthorized, and revitalized. *NOVA Newsletter, 12,* 1-5.

Stenson, K., & Cowell, D. (Eds.). (1991). *The politics of crime control.* London: Sage.

Stop drugs at the source. (1986, August 25). *U.S. News & World Report,* p. 19.

Storrie, K., & Poon, N. (1991). Programs for abusive men: A socialist-feminist perspective. In L. Samuelson & B. Schissel (Eds.), *Criminal justice: Sentencing issues and reform* (pp. 329-350). Toronto: Garamond.

Strauss, M. (1988, January). Sexual inequality = domestic violence. *USA Today, 116* (no. 2512), p. 8.

Street crime: People fight back. (1985, April 15). *U.S. News & World Report,* pp. 42-43.

Strick, A. (1979). *Injustice for all.* New York: Penguin.

Strickman, A. (1990, August 15). CAMP fires burn on. *Village Voice,* p. 17.

Striking at the source. (1986, July 28). *Time,* pp. 12-14.

Stroman, C., & Seltzer, R. (1985). Media use and perceptions of crime. *Journalism Quarterly, 62,* 340-345.

Taylor, I. (1981). *Law and order: Arguments for socialism.* London: Macmillan.

The criminal is living in a golden age. (1965, November 1). *U.S. News & World Report,* pp. 80-82.

The flames of fear. (1987, December 7). *U.S. News & World Report,* pp. 20-22.

Theft-proofing your car. (1988, February 22). *U.S. News & World Report,* p. 89.

The illusion of victim rights. (1989, March). *American Bar Association Student Lawyer,* pp. 1-4.

The public fights back. (1987, June 29). *U.S. News & World Report,* pp. 16-17.

Tidwell, M. (1989, July). Murder capital. *The Progressive,* p. 46.

Tifft, L., & Markham, L. (1991). Battering women and battering Central Americans. In H. Pepinsky & R. Quinney (Eds.), *Criminology as peacemaking* (pp. 114-153). Bloomington: Indiana University Press.

Tifft, L., & Sullivan, D. (1980). *The struggle to be human: Crime, criminology and anarchism.* Sanday, UK: Cienfuegos Press.

Tips on how to spot counterfeit goods. (1986, February 10). *U.S. News & World Report,* p. 52.

Tomasic, R., & Feeley, M. (Eds.). (1982). *Neighborhood justice*. New York: Longman.

Treaster, J. (1992, June 14). Twenty years of war on drugs, and no victory yet. *New York Times*, p. 7E.

Trebach, A. (1990, Summer). Accepting the presence of drugs. *New Perspectives Quarterly*, pp. 40-44.

Trotter, K. A. (1987). Compensating victims of terrorism. *Texas International Law Journal, 22*, 383-401.

Turpin, J., & Elias, R. (Eds). (1992, Fall). Why violence? *Peace Review*, pp. 1-48.

Tushnet, M. (1988). *Central America and the law*. Boston: South End.

Udovitch, M. (1991, December 24). Fear and loathing in Palm Beach. *Village Voice*, pp. 39-45.

Umbreit, M. (1985a). *Crime and reconciliation*. Nashville, TN: Abingdon.

Umbreit, M. (1985b). Victim-offender mediation and judicial leadership. *Judicature, 69*, 202-204.

Umbreit, M. (1986). Victim-offender mediation: A national survey. *Federal Probation, 50*, 53-56.

U.N. commission proposes action to prohibit violence against women. (1991, June). *United Nations Chronicle*, pp. 68-69.

United Nations Secretariat. (1980). *Crime and the abuse of power: Offenses and offenders beyond the reach of the law*. U.N. Doc.A/CONF/87/6. New York: Author.

U.S. mission: Cut off drugs at the source. (1986, July 28). *U.S. News & World Report*, p. 55.

Valverde, M. (1985). *Sex, power and pleasure*. Toronto: Women's Press.

Vankin, J. (1991). *Conspiracies, cover-ups and crimes*. New York: Paragon House.

Varenchik, R. (1987). Tell it to the judge. *California Lawyer, 7*, 9-12.

Vass, A. (1990). *Alternatives to prison*. London: Sage.

Vergara, C. J. (1990, March 27). Rebuilding drug city. *Village Voice*, pp. 25-29.

Viano, E. (1987). Victim's rights and the Constitution. *Crime & Delinquency, 33*, 438-451.

Viano, E. (1989). *Crime and its victims*. New York: Hemisphere.

Victim rights bill fuels get-tough stand. (1982). *American Bar Association Journal, 68*, 530-539.

Victim rights laws sometimes bring frustration, survey finds. (1987, December). *Criminal Justice Newsletter, 18*, 3-4.

Victims of crime. (1989, July 31). *U.S. News & World Report*, pp. 16-19.

Victims of Crime Resource Center. (1988). *Statutes of 1988 pertaining to crime victims*. Sacramento, CA: Author.

Video vigilantes. (1991, July 22). *Newsweek*, pp. 42-47.

Villmoare, E., & Neto, V. V. (1987, August). Victim appearances at sentencing under California's Victims' Bill of Rights. *Research in Brief*, pp. 1-5.

Vogel, R. D. (1983, March). Capitalism and incarceration. *Monthly Review*, pp. 30-41.

Wahrhaftig, P. (1979). Citizen dispute resolution. In R. O. Darnell, Else, & Wright (Eds.), *Alternatives to Prison* (pp. 92-99). Iowa City: University of Iowa School of Social Work.

Walker, S. (1982, October). What have civil liberties ever done for crime victims? Plenty! *Academy of Criminal Justice Sciences Today*, pp. 4-5.

Walker, S. (1985). *Sense and nonsense about crime*. Belmont, CA: Brooks/Cole.

Walklate, S. (1990). *Victimology*. Winchester, MA: Unwin-Hyman.

Wanted: Noriega. (1988, February 15). *Time*, pp. 16-17.

War by other means. (1990, February 10). *The Economist*, p. 50.

War on crime—by fed-up citizens. (1975, March 3). *U.S. News & World Report*, p. 38.

Warr, M. (1990). Dangerous situations: Social context and fear of victimization. *Social Forces, 68*, 891-907.

Weinstein, H., & Jones, C. (1990, March 25). Busted for life. *San Francisco Examiner*, p. 3.

Weisband, E. (Ed.). (1989). *Poverty amidst plenty.* Boulder, CO: Westview.

Welling, S. N. (1987). Victim participation in plea bargains. *Washington University Law Quarterly, 65,* 301-356.

Welsh, M. (1990, January 25). Close encounters: Inmates face their victims. *Sacramento News,* pp. 12-14.

We need drastic measures. (1989, March 13). *Newsweek,* p. 21.

Wenner, J. S. (1990, July 12). The war on drugs: Our next Vietnam. *Rolling Stone,* p. 11.

Wenz, E. P. (1989). America's new witch hunt. *San Francisco Weekly, 8* (33), 1, 6.

Wertheimer, R. (1991). Preferring punishment of criminals over providing for victims. In D. Sank & D. Caplin (Eds.), *To be a victim* (pp. 78-84). New York: Plenum.

Weston, B. (1987). The Reagan administration versus international law. *Case Western Journal of International Law, 19,* 295-302.

What about the victims of crime? (1975, February 24). *U.S. News & World Report,* p. 43.

What crime does to the victims. (1982, March 23). *Time,* pp. 29-30.

What the police can and cannot do about crime. (1970, July 13). *Time,* pp. 34-36.

What to do about crime in the U.S. (1967, August 7). *U.S. News & World Report,* pp. 70-73.

When citizens mobilize against crime. (1980, January 21). *U.S. News & World Report,* pp. 49-51.

When the guilty go free. (1989, May 22). *U.S. News & World Report,* p. 84.

When the police blunder a little. (1982, March 1). *Newsweek,* p. 37.

White, L. C. (1988). *Merchants of death: The American tobacco industry.* New York: William Morrow.

White fear, black crime. (1979, October 23). *U.S. News & World Report,* p. 134.

Whitman, S. (1992, May). The crime of black imprisonment. *Z Magazine,* pp. 69-72.

Why criminals go free: Revolving door justice. (1976, May 10). *U.S. News & World Report,* pp. 36-40.

Why justice can't be done. (1989, May 29). *Newsweek,* pp. 36-37.

Wideman, J. E. (1984). *Brothers and keepers.* New York: Penguin.

Williams, C. (1990). *Race against crack.* San Francisco: KQED Special Report.

Williams, H., & Murphy, P. V. (1990, January). The evolving strategy of police: A minority view. *NIJ Perspectives on Policing,* pp. 1-15.

Williams, T. (1990, Summer). Cocaine kids: the underground American dream. *New Perspectives Quarterly,* pp. 21-25.

Willis, B. L. (1984). State compensation of victims of violent crimes: The Council of Europe Convention of 1983. *Virginia Journal of International Law, 25,* 211-247.

Willis, E. (1989). Hell no, I won't go: End the war on drugs. *Village Voice* (September 19), pp. 29-32.

Wilson, J. Q. (1975). *Thinking about crime.* New York: Vintage.

Wilson, J. Q., & Herrnstein, R. (1985). *Crime and human nature.* Cambridge, MA: Harvard University Press.

Wishnu, S. (1989, April 5). As Crime takes over the city streets, where is the left? *The Guardian,* p. 19.

Wisotsky, S. (1986). *Breaking the impasse in the war on drugs.* Westport, CT: Greenwood.

Witkin, G., & Cuneo, A. Z. (1990, January 14). One step ahead of the law. *This World,* pp. 10-11.

Wolfe, A. (1978). *The seamy side of democracy.* New York: Longman.

Wolfe, L. (1991). *Violence against women.* Washington, DC: Center for Women's Policy Studies.

Woodiwiss, M. (1990). Crime crusades and corruption. *American Journal of Sociology, 96* (3), 798-799.

Wozencraft, K. (1990). *Rush.* New York: Random House.

Wright, J. D., & Sheley, J. F. (1992, Fall). Teenage violence and the urban underclass. *Peace Review*, pp. 26-29.

Wright, L. (1990, March 19). Farrakhan's mission: Fighting the drug war his way. *Newsweek*, p. 25.

Wright, M. (1985). The impact of victim-offender mediation on the victim. *Victimology, 10*, 630-646.

Wright, M. (1991). *Justice for victims and offenders: A restorative response to crime.* Philadelphia: Open University Press.

Wright, M., & Galaway, B. (1989). *Mediation and criminal justice: Victims, offenders & community.* Newbury Park, CA: Sage.

ya Salaam, K. (1988, September). Drug frenzy is nothing new in the U.S. *New Orleans Tribune*, pp. 6-7.

Yoffe, E. (1990, February-March). How to legalize. *Mother Jones*, pp. 18-19.

Young, M. (1989). The National Organization for Victim Assistance. In R. C. Monk (Ed.), *Taking sides: Clashing views on controversial issues in crime and criminology* (310-319). Guilford, CT: Dushkin.

Zalaquett, J. (1981). *The human rights issue and the human rights movement.* Geneva: World Council of Churches.

Zappa, V. (1990, April 23). America's drug children. *Daily Californian*, p. 9.

Zehr, H. (1990). *Changing lenses.* Scottsdale, PA: Herald.

Zimring, F., & Hawkins, G. (1989). *What kind of drug war?* Berkeley, CA: Earl Warren Legal Institute.

Zinn, H. (1984). *The twentieth century: A people's history.* New York: Harper & Row.

Zinn, H. (1990). *Declarations of independence.* New York: Harper Collins.

Index

About the Author

Robert Elias is Professor of Politics and chair of the Legal Studies and Peace and Justice Studies programs at the University of San Francisco (USF). He has taught at the University of California at Berkeley, the University of Maryland (Europe and College Park), The Pennsylvania State University, and Tufts University. He has been a researcher at the Vera Institute of Justice, the Center for the Study of Law and Society, and the International Institute of Human Rights. He is the author of *The Politics of Victimization*, *Victims of the System*, and *New Culture, Less Crime*, and he is coeditor of *The Peace Resource Book* and *Rethinking Peace*. He is now writing books on political music (*More Than the Melody*) and political exiles (*Alienated Americans at Home and Abroad*). He is the editor of *Peace Review*, a member of the editorial boards of *New Political Science* and the *International Review of Victimology*, and an associate editor of *Radical America*. He was awarded a Fulbright Grant to teach human rights in Sri Lanka, and he recently held the National Endowment for the Humanities chair in the Literature of Repression at USF.